WITCHCRAFT FOR HEALING

PATTI WIGINGTON

Witchcraft
for
Healing

RADICAL SELF-CARE FOR YOUR MIND, BODY, AND SPIRIT

**ROCKRIDGE
PRESS**

For general information on our other products and services or to obtain technical support, please contact our Customer Care Department within the United States at (866) 744-2665, or outside the United States at (510) 253-0500.

Rockridge Press publishes its books in a variety of electronic and print formats. Some content that appears in print may not be available in electronic books, and vice versa.

Interior and Cover Designer: Brieanna Hattey Felschow
Art Producer: Samantha Ulban
Editor: Emily Angell
Production Editor: Mia Moran

All images used under license © Sundra/CreativeMarket, Olgakoelsch/CreativeMarket, and Shutterstock

Author photo courtesy of Aaron Werner/Werner Entertainment

ISBN: Print 978-1-64739-793-7 | eBook 978-1-64739-478-3

R0

FOR ALL THE RADICAL,
SUBVERSIVE, WILD WOMEN
IN MY WORLD.

YOU KNOW
WHO YOU ARE.

CONTENTS

ꟼNTRODUCTION

Life is chaotic, isn't it? You probably spend so much time running from place to place, from obligation to obligation, that you miss how that busyness impacts you, on a spiritual, physical, and emotional level. But the busier we get, the more we neglect ourselves. That's why embracing a philosophy of radical self-care is so important.

I've been a practicing witch for more than three decades. Over the years, my practice has evolved significantly, and in entirely positive ways. I have worked magic for prosperity, healing, protection, and all kinds of other goals. When I first found myself drawn to witchcraft, I was at a point in my life where I had no clear sense of direction. I was struggling financially, I had no goals or life plan to speak of, and I was spending a lot of time with people who ultimately made me question my self-worth. It was time for change. Magical practice taught me the focus and self-discipline I needed to get back on track.

I learned early on that there was no limit to the ways I could help myself and improve my life by practicing witchcraft. It wasn't just that I could help myself directly by performing magic; it was also that magic's transformative, empowering nature allowed me to develop skills I needed to be successful in other, non-magical aspects of my life.

Except, for a while, I stopped helping myself. I got wrapped up in my family, jobs (often more than one at a time), and community work. I didn't want to be selfish, so I put everything I had into other people. I spent so much of my time and energy focusing on the needs of others that I lost track of who I really was. It's easy to lose your sense of who you are, and what your purpose is in the world, when you're defined only by your relationships—being someone's mother, spouse, or child. For women in particular, who are often societally conditioned to put the needs of family over their own desires and wants, this can be soul-crushing.

Eventually, I went back to focusing on my magic. But this time, I approached it from the radical notion that I deserved better from, and for, myself. I worked magic focused on developing my self-confidence, my divinatory skills, and my intuitive gifts. I dove into studying and research, learning about witchcraft and magic of the past. I also realized that I needed non-magical things that were *mine*—activities that didn't revolve around my spouse or my kids—and so I began to find ways to explore who I was as an individual, rather than being defined solely as someone's wife or mother.

And it worked. I figured out that this act of radical self-care was the best thing I could have done, not just for myself, but also for everyone around me. It improved my relationships as well as the way I felt about life itself.

Engaging in self-care means reclaiming your time and energy, and approaching life in a more mindful way. The term "self-care" has become trendy lately, and for some people, it simply means treating yourself to a bubble bath, indulging in some hardcore retail therapy, or snarfing down a gallon of ice cream while you watch a movie. For others, it means focusing primarily on exercise, healthy eating habits, and treating oneself to nice things now and then. But there's so much more to self-care. Radical self-care means making the quality of your own life a top priority, by making changes that impact not only the body and mind, but also the spirit.

Radical self-care is subversive because you put *yourself* first. Instead of focusing on all the things other people want from you—as many of us have been taught to do our entire lives—you set your sights on your own needs. Self-care isn't selfish at all; it's transformative. And how better to transform than with a bit of magic?

This book is designed for anyone who wants to reclaim their power and rebuild their life from the ground up. You don't have to be an experienced witch like me to perform the spells and rituals in this book—and there are no spiritual prerequisites, either. All you need is a desire to eliminate that which no longer serves you and embrace what does, while working to make your life more satisfying.

We'll kick off with a look at the history of witchcraft, exploring why it lends itself so perfectly to radical self-care. We'll learn some of the basic knowledge you need to approach your magic with confidence. Then we'll dive right into spells and rituals to help heal your mind, body, and spirit, as well as enrich your home and your community.

Let's rebel against a world that says that your needs don't matter, that the best thing you can do with your life is focus completely on the desires of others. Let's explore radical self-care, so you can embrace a life that's happy, healthy, and whole.

The Healing Roots of Witchcraft

In this chapter, you'll learn the basics of practicing magic and witchcraft with confidence. If you're new to this practice, you might wonder what magic and witchcraft actually entail. Magic is the ability to influence events, people, or issues deliberately through the use of metaphysical principles. Witchcraft is the practice of magic and ritual—often involving elements of the natural world—that are designed to bring about both small and large changes in the universe. Every person's magical practice is different, but probably includes some—or all—of these common elements: rituals, spellwork, prayer to your gods and goddesses, divination, a deep connection to the natural world, and an acknowledgment that the divine can be found in anything and anyone. All of these aspects, blended together, combine to create a practice in which you can manipulate both natural and supernatural forces to attain your desired goals and outcomes.

Whether you've been practicing for 10 years or 10 minutes, this chapter will provide you with a foundation of knowledge that you'll use throughout the book. You'll explore a very brief history of witchcraft, and discover how and why healing has become such a crucial focus of magical practice. You'll learn about the physical, emotional, and spiritual principles behind healing, and about the power found in the execution of spells and rituals. Finally, you'll look at some of the valuable lessons you can learn—and share with others—when you practice witchcraft for radical self-care to heal your mind, body, and spirit.

A Brief History of Witchcraft

It's safe to say that modern magical practice has roots in healing traditions that go back for ages. Tens of thousands of years ago, humans developed the belief system known as animism, which involved assigning a spirit to any person, animal, rock, tree, or other living thing. Animism eventually evolved into shamanism. A shaman is a practitioner who has direct access to the spirit world, practices divination, and uses supernatural forces to heal or protect their community. The practice of shamanism, which includes trance-work and ritual, is found in many cultures globally.

Ancient healers discovered that different herbs could cure certain illnesses, and utilized them in their healing practices. This formed the foundation of the witchcraft that is still practiced today. Although the delivery methods have changed somewhat—after all, a Paleolithic shaman couldn't order his favorite herbs online—the principles of magic remain similar to those employed by ancient shamans.

As secretive religious schools evolved in places like ancient Greece, the Roman Empire, and Mesopotamia, people began performing secret rituals in honor of their gods. Magic in this time period was often centered on healing the bodies and souls of those who were ill. The Indo-European world soon flourished, and priests and priestesses performed divination, banished evil spirits, created charms, and communicated with the spirits. They contributed vital services to the well-being of their communities. Many of these practices eventually came to form the cornerstone of magical practice in the Middle Ages, which in turn shaped the roots of the witchcraft that is performed by modern practitioners.

Witchcraft Through the Ages

The medieval period in Europe was a dark time for witches. The world was decimated by the bubonic plague, or Black Death, which killed anywhere from 75 to 200 million people in Europe and Asia, and all of a sudden, witches weren't as popular anymore. This devastating pandemic sparked rumors that witches were the cause of illness, disease, and death, which were the catalyst for several hundred years of persecution by the church and individuals alike. Although most of the people accused of witchcraft in Europe at this time actually weren't practicing witches, it was considered a crime nonetheless, and those who were found guilty were burned at the stake. In North America, people convicted of witchcraft were hanged.

Magic went underground for centuries, and those who practiced it did so in secret, studying mystical arts in small groups sworn to silence. It arose again in the late 19th century, when it suddenly became popular and trendy. Over the next few decades, witchcraft re-emerged into the mainstream, and by the mid-20th century, witches were practicing publicly in the United States and elsewhere. Today, witches are out in full force, working for their communities and fighting for social change, much like their ancestors might have done.

While Wicca is the best-known of the modern witchcraft belief systems, there are other forms, including eclectic, kitchen witchcraft, and hedge witchery. And though much has changed in the world since the era of those early shamans, many contemporary witches have practices based on the traditions of ancient folk magic.

Popular Myths and Misconceptions

Old beliefs die hard, and thanks to lingering inaccuracies, there are still plenty of myths and misconceptions about witchcraft and those who practice it.

Myth: Witches worship the devil.

Fact: The devil, or Satan, is a Christian construct, and most people practicing witchcraft today don't identify as Christian. Even among those who do, the devil doesn't play a part in magical work, because witchcraft is focused on things like healing, protection, abundance, and personal growth—none of which really fits into the devil's domain.

Myth: Witchcraft involves dramatic magical powers, like making a physical object disappear or change.

Fact: Real magic—actual, hands-on witchcraft—is nothing like you see in the movies or on television. Harry Potter might be able to conjure up a chocolate frog out of nowhere, and the sisters of *Charmed* can change their eye color with the flick of a wand, but that's not how real witchcraft works. Instead, it utilizes the will and intent of the practitioner to bring about change.

Myth: Witchcraft is evil.

Fact: Although there are certainly some religions that are convinced it's bad, the people practicing witchcraft today are often doing so for the greater good. They're performing healing magic, bringing prosperity into their own lives, building community, and empowering themselves to live their best lives. If those things are evil, well, then I don't want to be good.

Myth: Witches frequently cast curses, hexes, or other negative spells.

Fact: Is it possible to use witchcraft for nefarious purposes? Sure. But the majority of modern practitioners agree it's a bad idea. If you believe that what goes around comes around, just imagine the sorts of things you'll invite into your life if you start performing negative magic! In addition, there are certain moral and ethical guidelines in many modern traditions that prohibit the use of harmful magic.

The Healing Tradition of Witchcraft

Despite what folktales tell us—that witches are mischievous, up to no good, and fattening up peasant children in order to cook them in a cauldron—most modern witchcraft is actually rooted in the long history of healing magic. In early societies, witches lived on the edge of town, tucked behind hedges and nestled in forests, practicing magic to help cure disease, prevent disasters, and bring prosperity to their communities.

The local witch might have a vast collection of herbs—some they grew themselves, others foraged from woods and meadows. If you struggled with health problems ranging from infertility to unwanted pregnancy, heartburn to hemorrhoids, a cough to mysterious aches and pains, the village witch handled it. They might brew a tea, craft a poultice, or perhaps burn some plants to heal the people who came to them for help.

Over time, magic and science blended together, and people realized that healing wasn't just the domain of the local witch—it was science. But while traditional herbal healing evolved into modern medicine, old traditions lingered. There are people still practicing healing witchcraft today—and they're healing their neighbors and communities. Today, the village witch still exists—but now, instead of living on the edge of town, she lives in a house in the suburbs, or a dorm room on your college campus. Instead of existing on the outskirts of society, today's witches are baristas, business people, lawyers, librarians, and everything in between. They're working to make the world better, encouraging self-care and empowerment, and carrying on a tradition that goes back for ages.

Healing the Individual

How can you use witchcraft to heal your soul, your spirit, and your body? In her groundbreaking book *The Life-Changing Magic of Tidying Up*, Marie Kondo encourages readers to get rid of things in their homes that no longer "spark joy." She's kind about it, suggesting you hold each item and thank it before getting rid of it. But what if, in addition to old clothes and broken dinnerware, you got rid of ways of thinking and behaving that didn't serve you? What if you said goodbye to unhealthy habits, toxic relationships, and negative mindsets, and welcomed freedom, power, and conscious emotional well-being? This is your opportunity to eliminate the negative from your life, and open up space for the positive. That's how we heal our minds and bodies to manifest real joy. That's what radical self-care is all about.

Healing the Community

You don't have to limit this to healing yourself. Why not use magic to heal the community around you? Things are tough right now; we're in a period of drastic social upheaval and our communities are broken. Maybe your community is a small town, or perhaps it's a big city. Maybe it's your college campus or local art scene. Perhaps it's simply the group of people you spend the most time with. Regardless of how you view community, healing witchcraft can make it better. As you heal yourself, draw on your own magic, and work to heal all that surrounds you.

Healing the World

Throughout the years, witches have actively worked on a vast number of worldwide issues. In fact, in the summer of 1940, a group of British witches performed a spell to keep Hitler's army from invading Britain, in a ritual that came to be known as "Operation Cone of Power." Today's witches are working as activists, resistance leaders, and catalysts of social change. They are facilitating conversations about hard topics like racism, misogyny, injustice, and oppression. They're doing all of these things by way of magical practice, in tandem with non-magical actions and community building. A spell could be performed for protection at a non-violent protest, and at the same time, organizers might be using spreadsheets to keep track of people's emergency contact information. The magical lives side by side with the mundane—or non-magical—as the community works together to bring about sweeping differences in the world.

Healing Through the Natural World

Our natural world is an amazing thing to experience. Who doesn't feel a sense of wonder at the sight of a vast mountain range, or the power of a raging storm? It's humbling, empowering, and awe-inspiring all at the same time, and it reminds us of our place in the universe.

That's why getting back to nature can often be a vital part of self-care, and subsequently self-healing, too. A 2011 scientific study by Catharine Ward Thompson and other researchers found that regular exposure to green spaces can lower the level of cortisol in your body. Because cortisol is a key stress hormone, the more time you spend outdoors, the lower you'll find your anxiety levels dropping. Walking in the woods, sitting barefoot in the grass, listening to primordial sounds, or just touching plants in your garden can normalize your blood pressure, slow your heart rate, and reduce tension. By making the deliberate choice to spend time in nature, you can create a balance for yourself, a holistic harmony that nourishes your spirit.

The natural world is also a magnificent source of magical energy. Whether you're working with herbs and crystals, the stars and the planets, or a stick you found during a walk in the woods, the natural world around us—in all its many shapes and forms—can serve as a catalyst and source of tremendous power.

GET BACK
TO NATURE

....

Spend time learning about herbs, trees, and stones. Hold a crystal in your hand, close your eyes, and feel its vibrations. Learn how your body responds to it. Plant herbs in your garden, or in a pot if you don't have a yard. Watch them emerge from the soil, new life beginning, and tend them as they grow. Smell them, feel them between your fingertips, and attune yourself to their energies. Find a tree, wrap your arms around it, and breathe deeply. Can you feel its power resonating into you? Study the cycles of the seasons and recognize how you respond—physically and emotionally—as the environment around you changes from month to month.

The Power of Spells and Rituals

When you perform a magical spell or ritual, you're carrying on a time-honored tradition that began before the start of recorded history. It doesn't matter if you're new to witchcraft or a veteran, if you learned about magic from reading books, attending classes, or sitting at a kitchen table with a mentor. What matters the most are intent and purpose.

Many people will tell you intent is *everything* when it comes to spellwork. And yes, intent is important—it's the end goal you hope to achieve by casting your spell or performing your ritual. But purpose—*why* you've set the goal—is just as valuable.

Magic has power. Whether you're performing a simple spell or an elaborate ritual, the end result is bringing about change and influencing the world around you. This is why it's crucial that you always consider not just what you're doing, but *why* you're doing it.

For instance, your intent might be to heal your body after an illness, but the purpose is so that you'll feel better and be able to enjoy activities like you used to. Perhaps the intent of your ritual is to bring bounty to a local food pantry, but the purpose is to reduce hunger and food inequality in your community. Keep both intent and purpose in mind during your workings.

Using Your Powers for Good

Witchcraft and other occult practices are seeing a revival these days; magic has almost gone mainstream. Because of this, there is a *lot* of information out there, and a lot of different types of people practicing witchcraft for a variety of different reasons. Some of those reasons might be less than positive, or even downright unpleasant. If you're interested in practicing witchcraft simply so you can hex your coworker who keeps stealing your sandwiches in the break room, or curse your landlord because he raised the rent, this might not be the book for you.

This book focuses on healing and self-care, and malevolence doesn't lend itself well to either of these things. For the purposes of the spells and rituals you'll find in the chapters that follow, we're only working on manifesting positive transformation. To paraphrase Elphaba and Glinda from the musical *Wicked*, you'll see change for good.

Healing Lessons from Witchcraft

Some people believe you can be born a witch, and others feel you become a witch simply by practicing witchcraft. Whichever is the case, anyone can learn how to practice witchcraft, and the valuable lessons that healing magic can teach us.

Witchcraft is focused on honoring your own divinity and strength. In a world where the deck is often stacked against us—particularly if you're female or of non-binary gender identity, a person of color, or LGBTQ+-identifying—you can practice in the ways that feel the most powerful to you. By reclaiming that sense of control, you can feel worthy and valued once again.

For anyone who has ever felt they were marginalized, oppressed, not enough, or perhaps too much, the empowerment that comes with magical practice is a potent form of self-healing. By taking back your sense of self through spells, rituals, and mindful practice, you can learn something pretty amazing: who you truly are. And once you meet that person, you get to celebrate them in all of their magical glory. As you heal yourself, you'll be able to do something even more spectacular, which is to share that sense of wholeness and joy with people around you. Radical self-care through witchcraft really is the gift that keeps on giving.

How Witchcraft Can Help You Heal Your Mind, Body, and Spirit

Magical practice is a great way to heal the mind. Whether you're doing regular meditation, drawing a daily Tarot card, or spending time outside under the full moon, witchcraft forces you to focus, breathe, ground and center yourself. Getting your head on straight also helps a lot when it comes to magic; if you're distracted and mentally erratic, that will affect the results of your magic.

Witchcraft can heal the body, as well. Got an illness, exhaustion, or anxiety running you down? See the doctor, then work up a spell to bring healing energy into your life. Although magic should never be used as a substitute for proper medical or mental health treatment, it can certainly be used in tandem with the mundane.

Finally, don't forget the power of witchcraft on your spirit. If a holistic approach to magic brings about change in the mind and body, then the soul is soon to follow. When you feel better physically and mentally, you'll see benefits on a spiritual level, as transformative healing goes full circle.

Awaken Your Inner Witch

If you accept that everyone has a little bit of magic inside them, then sometimes it's a matter of just waking it up. But how do you begin?

One of the most vital steps is to remain open-minded. Even though there is no scientific or logical reason for magic to work, the fact remains that it does, and has for centuries. As you expand your studies, exploring divination, spirit communication, spellwork, or any other aspect of witchcraft and magic, you'll soon see how it is all interconnected—even when there's no rational explanation for it.

Draw out your inner witch by honoring your personal power. This isn't easy to do if you're accustomed to giving your power away to other people. But if you learn to set boundaries, exercise a strong sense of free will, and open yourself up to introspection, it can happen. Listen to the ideas and thoughts of others, but don't let anyone tell you what to believe or feel.

In addition, as Spider-Man often reminds us, "With great power comes great responsibility." That means you—and you alone—are the one who has to own your actions, good or bad, and accept the consequences, whatever they are. While this might sound a little intimidating, it's not a bad thing. It can keep you in check and serve as a cautionary reminder that what you do and say will come back to you in some way or form. Stick to doing positive manifestation, and you should see positive results in return.

Cleansing and Purification

Purification and cleansing are handy tools in the witch's arsenal. A purification is an active and deep metaphysical purge of negative energy, while cleansing is more a form of preventive maintenance. There are several different methods you can use to cleanse or purify a space.

- Herbs or plants can be burned to send negativity away into the universe via the smoke. Use sweetgrass, sage, or any other blend of herbs and plants.
- Asperging is a method by which liquid—water, wine, or milk blended with honey—is sprinkled around an area to purify it.
- A bowl of sea salt, scattered around an area, is a great way to purify a space.
- Use fire to purify by lighting a candle and walking in a clockwise direction, or placing candles at the cardinal points—north, east, south, and west—when you perform rituals or spellwork.

Conclusion

Is witchcraft easy? Not always. There will be times when you find yourself stepping out of your comfort zone. You might find spells and rituals and actions in the coming chapters that make you question whether they're worth the effort and work involved. And for you personally, they might not be. But then again, if you're willing to read this book in the first place, it's because you decided it was time to take some sort of healing, self-transformative action. As you work your magic, you'll find a renewed sense of empowerment, balance, and well-being, all on your journey to crafting a life that's happy, healthy, and whole.

In the next chapter, we'll talk about what radical self-care actually entails, its benefits, and why it ties into witchcraft. We'll explore the connection between the mind, body, and spirit, and talk about the importance and value of setting goals and magical intentions. We'll learn how radical self-care can improve our self-esteem, boost our creative spirit, and help our relationships become more rewarding.

Before you turn the page, close your eyes, take a deep breath, and remind yourself that your peace of mind and sense of well-being are valuable. Acknowledge that you matter and are important, and that it's okay for you to want your needs to be met. Understand that the happier you are, the more vibrant and joyful your life will become.

Now, let's get radical.

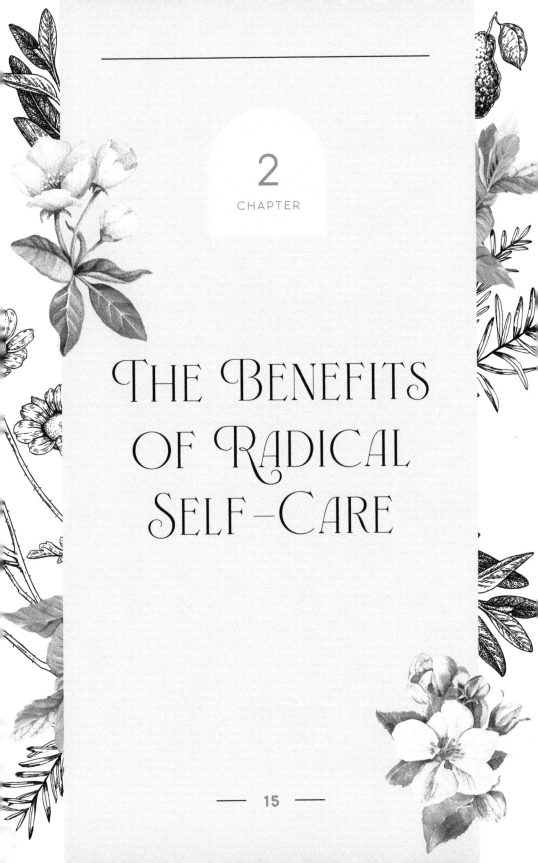

The Benefits of Radical Self-Care

"Self-care" is a popular buzzword these days. You can't open a magazine without reading about the benefits of a spa day or a girls' night out. But self-care is much more than a manicure or retail therapy. This chapter will break down the concept of self-care, and why it's not selfish. You'll learn how radical self-care can benefit you long-term, and guide you toward a sense of fulfillment. You'll also learn about ways to set your personal healing goals, the power of setting boundaries and asking for help, and the radical act of expressing gratitude.

What Is Radical Self-Care?

Self-care is about working on various aspects of your life from a self-empowering mindset, and gradually working toward a life that's whole and healthy. How you care for yourself physically and mentally has a profound effect on the way you interact with others, as well as how you view life and the world. When you're already prioritizing well-being, you're more likely to have strong and healthy coping mechanisms for dealing with loss, trauma, or other potentially overwhelming experiences. It takes a lot of energy to rebuild your life when the world is falling apart, and if you're exhausted and angry all the time, it's easy to feel like you're running on empty.

Radical, transformative self-care is the crazy, wonderful idea that it's acceptable to take care of yourself first, so that you can give your attention to others in a way that's healthy. When you're on an airplane, the flight attendant explains that if there's an emergency, you should put your own oxygen mask on first, and then help others with theirs. Nurturing your own spirit, in whatever ways work best for you, is the first step to create the ability to care for others and live wholeheartedly. Grab your own oxygen mask first.

It's Not All Bubble Baths and Adaptogenic Mushroom Lattes

For some people, the simple act of taking a bath, drinking a fancy coffee, or buying cute shoes is the pinnacle of self-care—and if that's all you need to rejuvenate yourself, that's wonderful. But for many of us, there's much more to self-care, including developing healthy, self-affirming habits.

Self-care is uniquely personal, and only you can decide how much of which things you need in your life. But there are some basics that benefit almost everyone.

- A solid amount of rest is crucial—try to follow a consistent sleep schedule so you're revitalized when you wake.

- Maintain a healthy diet full of as many nourishing foods as you can manage.

- Try to stay physically active, if you have the ability and the resources.

- Learn to set and maintain boundaries in your relationships, both personal and professional.

- Practice whatever techniques you can for stress management, whether it's yoga, gardening, meditation, or axe-throwing.

- Find a way to achieve the work-life balance that works best for you.

The Connection between Witchcraft and Radical Self-Care

Practicing witchcraft is itself an act of radical self-care—it's the use of will and energy to bring about positive change. It's the chance to own our mistakes and take responsibility for our happiness, to no longer feel constrained by the world's boundaries, and to set our own guidelines for how we are treated and how we treat others. Witchcraft is an opportunity to use positive manifestation to craft a life that is happy, healthy, and whole—and to share that bounty with those around us.

When you learn how to use magic, energy, and will to create space for yourself and for those who are vulnerable, you can engage in some of the most profound self-care acts of all. You can focus on your own needs and desires when society tells you to sit down, shut up, be polite, and put others ahead of yourself. That is some pretty subversive witchcraft.

The Importance of Self-Care for Holistic Healing

Why is self-care such a big deal when it comes to holistic healing? Holistic healing focuses on treating the whole self—the body, mind, and spirit—in a quest for optimal well-being. Subsequently, self-care begins with developing a sense of how interconnected all things are in this great big web we call the universe. When we heal one part of our life, it helps heal the other parts as well. Creating a ripple effect, a healthy mindset is something we can share with others, without losing anything in the process. After all, wellness isn't pie—you don't miss out by giving a piece to someone else.

Arin Murphy-Hiscock says in *The Witch's Book of Self-Care* that self-care is a complex system of regular, small acts that all work together to create a life that feels worthy. But it's also an attitude shift. By consciously changing your mindset to understand that you are worthy and important, you'll change the way other people view you—and the way you allow them to treat you. By cultivating a life full of people who see you as having value, you'll find that your relationships become richer and bring you more joy, which makes you happier overall.

Furthermore, a shift in your mindset and overall attitude can help you improve the life you're living and aim for goals that unlock your fullest potential. When life improves, and you achieve your dreams, you feel better emotionally and spiritually—and that can help you feel better physically. It all ties together. That's the holistic value of the freedom of self-care.

The Mind, Body, Spirit Connection

You aren't defined by any one thing. You're not just the size of your hips, your ability to bang out a mile on the treadmill, your anxiety disorder, your job, or your role as a parent or partner. You're so much more than any single attribute—you are a wondrous combination of all the things that blend together to make you unique. This is why it's important to understand the connection between the mind, body, and spirit. These three aspects of the human self are always intertwined, and healing one helps facilitate healing the others.

Think for a moment about the last time you were really anxious about something. You probably experienced an elevated heart rate, and maybe your palms were sweaty. Perhaps you thought about meditating to calm down, but you were so worked up that you couldn't focus. Your anxiety affected not only your mind, but also your body and spirit. With radical self-care, you'll tap into this connection between the different parts of your being and develop the ability to heal yourself—all the varied components of you—from the inside out.

Healing from the Inside Out

What does "healing from the inside out" mean? It's the idea that healing must take place in your mind and spirit before it can manifest on the outside. How do you achieve this? It starts with creating a deliberate sense of self-awareness. In other words, you have to identify the problem at hand. You'll also need to figure out what your own role in the problem is. For instance, if you're frustrated with a coworker, that's a problem. But if your frustration is because you've failed to communicate your own boundaries to that coworker, then you've played a role in creating the problem.

If you're not sure exactly what the root of the matter is, it's okay to ask someone you trust for input. We all have that friend who tells us what we need to hear, even when it's not what we *want* to hear—pull that person in for feedback.

Finally, ask yourself what you can do differently. This is hard for some people, because most of us determine what we *can* do based upon what we think others will *let* us do. This is why setting intentions and goals is such a valuable part of self-care.

The Role of Manifestations and Setting Intentions

Let's talk for a moment about the importance of manifestation when it comes to self-care. Manifestation, in a spiritual context, is what happens when our dreams, goals, and wishes become reality through our own efforts, either magical or otherwise. Because self-care places an emphasis on positive, trans-formative change, there's value to be found in moving toward your new reality and manifesting those intentions that make you feel complete and whole.

Manifestation doesn't mean you're going to snap your fingers—or wave a wand—and *poof,* all of your wishes are fulfilled or your problems suddenly vanish into thin air. Rather, it is an ongoing, gradual transformation, as you work toward the changes you desire.

Setting your intention is the first step to making manifestation happen. It's where you determine your clear goals, acknowledge what you want, and figure out how to get it. Once you've set your intention, it's time to get to work, whether it's by way of ritual, spellwork, or mundane actions—and often, you can accomplish a lot with a combination of all three.

Manifesting a goal is the long-term result of taking charge. Though some people believe that all you have to do to manifest things is to visualize what you want, the truth is that you have to act—if you don't, nothing will ever be different. You can't sit around waiting for things to happen, or for other people to start treating you differently.

I've found that a key aspect of manifesting is what comes afterward: gratitude. By expressing thankfulness for the things that you manifest—including the things you're finally able to release and purge—you open up the doors for even more good stuff to come your way.

Get Clear on Your Healing Goals

In a way, setting a goal is a magical act. It's the first step on your way to manifesting what you want, whether that's health, abundance, or just plain old peace of mind. Many people find it's better to start off small, at least when you're beginning. While it's admirable to set a goal of losing 50 pounds, it may be easier if you focus on losing the first 10, then another 10, and so on.

It's also a good idea to keep things basic. If your goal is to run a 5K someday, but you're too worn out at the end of the day to even go for a walk, focus on a simpler approach. Start by setting the goal of blocking out time to walk around the block. Once you're doing that on a regular basis, move toward building up endurance. Soon, you'll be walking a mile, then two, and three. Eventually, you'll be running them.

Set your goals based on "Me" and "I" statements. Target your intentions on your own behavior and responses. For instance, rather than telling your partner, "You never watch the kids so I can go to the gym," try reframing it as, "Improving my health is a big goal for me, so I need to work out without the kids." If you tend to snap at your teen and say, "You didn't call last night when you were running late," instead try something like, "When I don't know where you are, it makes me feel really helpless and anxious."

Keep in mind that when you're goal setting, you also need to make sure you're reaching for what *you* want. Are you trying to live up to the expectations of others at your own expense? Set goals for things that you know will make you happy and follow your own dreams.

Self-Love

There's an old saying that if you don't love yourself, no one will love you. However, it's completely possible to be loved by others even when you feel completely unlovable. But if you develop a sense of self-love, you can recognize you're *worthy* of being loved, and improve the way others love you.

A solid sense of self-love also creates the ability to make choices that serve your well-being and nurture your spirit. It makes it so much easier for you to set boundaries—both personal and professional—by communicating that you value and respect yourself. The way you treat yourself lays the foundation for the way others treat you in return. Why not allow yourself to feel like you matter to the world?

Radical self-care is a great way to cultivate self-love. It can help you realize that not only are you pretty awesome, but also that your value isn't determined by the opinions of others.

Peace of Mind

There's a degree of peace of mind that comes with radical self-care. It's the knowledge that no matter what kind of curveballs life throws your way, you're emotionally, physically, and spiritually equipped to handle them. Developing healthy coping strategies before you actually need to use them is one of the most powerful side effects of regular self-care practices. Knowing how you'll respond to something ahead of time prepares you for the next crisis, and being prepared means you'll be able to wrangle whatever it is in a way that isn't self-destructive.

Again, everyone's barometer is different, so for some people, peace of mind is found through meditation or prayer. For others, it's through physical activities. Maybe for you, it's discovered via creative outlets. Whatever your peace of mind source is, embrace it, and let it guide you.

Your Creative Spirit

What's your creative outlet? Does painting, writing, or welding get your creative juices flowing? Maybe you like to walk in the woods, gathering up found items to use in crafts or sculptures. Perhaps you carve wood, cross-stitch, or bead jewelry. There's something incredibly meditative about the act of making something from scratch, so no matter what your creative spark may be, you can utilize it for healing.

Creative people tend to be emotionally invested in the world around them. They feel more, they're empathetic and compassionate, and they see things with a depth and clarity that not everyone experiences. Because of this, they're also more vulnerable emotionally; look at all of the artists throughout history whose work expressed their anxiety, fear, and pain. That's why it makes sense to invest deeply in radical self-care.

With radical self-care, the creative spirit is nourished. The better you feel, the more you create. And the more you create, the better you feel.

Stronger Boundaries

You know that setting boundaries is important. Making a decision like refusing to take on a workload that harms your mental health, or resisting a friend who constantly asks you to solve all her problems, improves your quality of life. However, most of us find it really hard to set boundaries— and once they've been set, maintaining them can be a challenge. After all, we're encouraged to be there for others in their times of need. It's hard to feel supportive toward other people when you're also saying no, right? And worse yet, if you set boundaries, people might think you don't value your relationships. You may feel like you constantly need to prove yourself by taking on the demands of others. So instead of setting boundaries, you probably often say "Yes," even though you're overwhelmed.

Radical self-care posits that setting boundaries is healthy for you, because your identity doesn't have to be tied up in how much stuff you do for others. Even though each of us has been socially conditioned to hustle and grind constantly, we do so at our own expense. By setting boundaries, you get to be more selective about what you do, who you do it with, and how much time and energy you invest.

Ask For Help

Effective leaders all have one thing in common: a willingness to surround themselves with motivated people who can help them when they need it. These competent people take on the tasks the leaders don't have the time, energy, or interest to tackle. If you're a leader, delegating is essential to self-care, too.

Asking for help can be challenging, because most of us have been conditioned to think we have to handle everything ourselves. Break that habit by asking yourself questions every time you feel compelled to tackle another duty. Do you have to be the one to bake all the cookies for the school fundraiser? Is it imperative that you do everyone else's laundry in the house? Do you have to be the one to organize yet another baby shower for a coworker? Ask others to take on tasks you can't handle. Here's a secret: most people love to help out. But they won't if you don't ask.

Better Relationships

Ever feel like you're giving your all and receiving nothing in return? Relationships aren't supposed to be transactional, but there's always some give and take. When you're tapped out and you've got nothing left to give, it's partly because you haven't intentionally taken the time to care for yourself. Self-care is an ongoing project, rather than a one-shot deal. Investing time and energy into doing whatever rejuvenates you is worthwhile, because it creates fulfilling, rewarding, positive habits. These extend into all of the other parts of your life, including your relationships with others. Whether it's your partner and kids, your friend circle, or your coworkers, you'll like them a lot better when you're feeling good on the inside.

Radical Self-Care for Your Mind, Body, Spirit, and Home

Self-care starts from within, so as you embrace more mindful practices, you'll start to see changes on mental, physical, and spiritual planes. You'll bring about a shift in your personal energy that leads to positive changes on many different levels. As you do, something even more magical will happen: you'll realize self-care can extend outward into your home and personal space.

Your living space is where you spend a good portion of your time—even if you have a full-time job, your home is the place you always return to. It's your spiritual retreat—or, at least, it should be—and it ought to be welcoming and warm, a place of calmness, joy, and good vibes. With radical self-care, you'll learn to craft an environment of positive energy that nurtures your spirit the moment you walk through the door.

Your home can become an extension of your true self and give you something to look forward to at the end of the day. Creating sacred space will help you eliminate elements of your surroundings that cause you stress, anxiety, or discomfort. After all, your home—whether it's a small apartment, a cabin in the woods, or a big sprawling mansion in the 'burbs—is your castle. Treat it accordingly.

An Attitude of Gratitude

Showing appreciation can make you feel happier, so consider making it your default setting. People who show gratitude often feel an overall sense of abundance, partly from recognizing the joy in small, simple pleasures, and partly because there's a belief that the more you show thankfulness, the more you'll have to be thankful for. Try these ways to acknowledge thankfulness:

- Keep a journal where you can jot down the things you're grateful for.
- Show others your appreciation by sending thank-you notes, leaving comment cards at businesses, or just telling someone what a great job they've done.
- Develop a mindset of charitable giving, to share your good fortune with those who have less.
- Recognize the people who inspire you to be better, and honor them.

Let's Get Started

We've discussed radical self-care, the ways it can benefit you, and the things you can learn from engaging in mindful self-care practices. Now what?

Here's the hard part. You have to make a commitment to yourself. You have to choose a shift in attitude, and embrace a mindful, conscious lifestyle and mentality that will benefit you on your journey toward healing. If you aren't ready right now, that's okay. It might be scary to step outside your comfort zone. But the sooner you get started on this new adventure of the self, the sooner you'll start to see results. Are you willing and able to say to yourself, "I deserve more, I am more, I matter," even if you think there's a chance you might fail?

Conclusion

Radical self-care sounds pretty, well, radical. After a lifetime of being told you must put the needs of others before your own or be considered selfish, here I am, telling you it's okay to focus inward for a while. On top of that, that it's *healthy*, too!

But it's true. A self-care mindset isn't a selfish one at all. Because in the long run, as you heal your mind, body, and spirit, you'll be able to extend that power outward, healing your home, your relationships, and even your community, both locally and globally. That's some pretty heavy stuff, isn't it?

In the next chapter, we'll dive into some of the healing tools of witchcraft that you can use as you embark on this magical new journey of radical transformation. We'll learn about connecting with nature and the seasons, as well as how to harness lunar and solar energy for your benefit. We'll talk about creating sacred space, and discover some of the material items used in manifesting spells and rituals for self-healing.

Are you ready to go make some magic?

HERBS, OILS, AND MOONLIGHT: THE HEALING TOOLS OF A WITCH

In this chapter, we're going to dive into some of the tools we can use to make magic. We're going to cover everything from divination methods to herbs, crystals, and essential oils. Do you have to gather up every single one of these magical tools to get started? Of course not—in fact, you don't technically need *any* of them. But tools help with focus. They provide a tangible delivery method to make magic happen.

Before You Start

If you're acquiring magical tools for the first time, take it slow. You don't have to run out and buy everything today. Instead, figure out which tools you're most likely to need, and then purchase one or two at a time, in order of importance. You may find it easiest to start with a few candles in different colors, symbols of the four elements, some herbs that speak to you, and a wand or athame—a magical knife—for directing energy. Otherwise, you'll have a pile of stuff gathering dust on your altar, untouched. Understand that magical tools are just *things*, after all, and that magic is made in the mind and the heart.

Connecting to Nature

Developing a connection to the natural world is a great way to tune in to your magical abilities. There are many different ways to connect to nature, so if you have the time and ability, spend an afternoon outdoors. Plant a garden or set up a birdhouse. Lay in your yard and watch the clouds drift above you in the sky. And you don't have to restrict your connection to just observing your own backyard. Learn about the changing world around you, and in your own neighborhood. Study the constantly shifting climate in whatever region you live.

Read on to learn more about some natural elements you'll work with in your spells. The more you get to know the natural world, the better you'll come to understand how to work with it in a magical context.

The Seasons

For many witches, the changing seasons play an integral role in how they engage with their magic. Our ancestors knew the shifting seasons indicated agricultural markers. When the ground got warmer, it was time to plant crops, and as the nights grew longer and cooler, it was harvest time. This knowledge was essential for their survival, and has carried over into witchcraft traditions today.

However, the seasons also matter because they can affect the energy around you. Spring is a great time to work magic related to new beginnings, freedom, fertility, and adventure. Summer is associated with passion and growth, action, and power. To work on dreams and emotions, divination or spirit communication, consider taking advantage of the energy of autumn. Finally, winter is the perfect season for prosperity and wealth, or magic related to the stability of the home.

The Elements

The four classical elements—earth, air, fire, and water—are often invoked in spellwork and ritual. You may find you connect to one of these more than others, or you could work with all of them based upon your magical goals. Earth is linked to security, stability, and the structure of the home. Air, connected to the soul and the breath of life, is related to communication, wisdom, and carrying away trouble. Fire is tied to passion, strong will, and energy—and the power to both create and destroy. Water is an element of emotions, healing, cleansing, and purification. In some magical belief systems, there is a fifth element, that of Spirit, representing the elusive cosmic whole of all life forms.

Solar Festivals

In many traditions of modern witchcraft, solar festivals are celebrated to mark both the spring and autumn equinoxes, when the hours of light and darkness are equal. They're also celebrated to mark the summer and winter solstices. The summer solstice, or midsummer, is the longest day of the year. It's a day of solar energy and power, when celebrations focus on growth, light, and the abundance of the land itself, as the sun begins its journey away from the earth. In contrast, the winter solstice, or Yule, is the longest night of the year, and it represents the return of the sun. It's a time marked by darkness, and there's a chill in the air, but there's the knowledge that the days will soon grow longer, making it a season of hope.

Equinoxes take place in spring and fall. Because these days contain an equal number of light and dark hours, they are often celebrations of harmony and balance.

You may feel more energized during major events like a solar eclipse. Use the sun's energy to consecrate and bless your magical tools. Place them outside on a bright, sunny day and leave them out until dusk. If you like, offer a simple incantation, such as "I call upon the magic of the sun to bless these items, and give them power."

The Phases of the Moon

In some magical practices, moon phases are an important part of spellwork. Each lunar phase—waxing, full, waning, and dark—has its own unique set of magical properties that make it an especially good time to perform certain types of spells. If you'd like to follow lunar cycles for your magic, the guidelines are pretty simple. For the waxing moon, when the moon grows from dark to full, perform magic focused on attracting things to you. During the full moon itself, do workings focusing on spiritual development and personal growth. As the moon wanes from full to dark, put your energy into baneful magic, eliminating and banishing things you want to remove from your life. Once the moon goes dark, take some time to cleanse and purify your body and mind, and do magic related to inner peace and harmony.

Herbs, Plants, Flowers, and Tea Leaves

Herbs and plants are a vital component of some magical practices, which makes sense because leaves and flowers like lemon balm, thistle, yarrow, and chamomile have long played a part in healing medicine. As you delve into healing magic, you'll find that it's useful to have both dried and fresh herbs and flowers—apple, comfrey, feverfew, hyssop, lavender, and peppermint are great ones to have on hand. You even might want to consider blending your own herbal teas to use in your practice. However, it's very important that you also have a trustworthy herbal reference book, to make sure that you don't accidentally ingest a plant that will make you sick. Scott Cunningham's *Encyclopedia of Magical Herbs* is a great place to start.

Stones, Crystals, and Gems

Crystals and gemstones will be valuable additions to your witchy tool kit. Each stone has its own unique energy vibration, and many are associated with healing magic. Agate, amethyst, hematite, jasper, clear quartz, and tiger's eye stones all have healing properties that you can include in your workings. Use them for anything from balancing your chakras and lifting your spirits to boosting mental acuity and shielding against illness.

PROPERTY/ PURPOSE/RITUAL	HERBS
BANISHING	Hyssop, Lilac, Pennyroyal, Rue
CALMING	Basil, Catnip, Lavender
CLEANSING AND PURIFICATION	Comfrey, Hyssop, Lavender, Sage, Sandalwood, Sweetgrass
DIVINATION AND SPIRIT COMMUNICATION	Basil, Comfrey, Dandelion, Mugwort
DREAMS	Lavender, Mugwort, Mullein, Vervain
HEALING	Apple, Comfrey, Feverfew, Hyssop, Lavender, Peppermint, Yarrow
INTUITION, MEDITATION, AND PSYCHIC DEVELOPMENT	Chamomile, Cinnamon, Mugwort, Sage, Sandalwood
CONFIDENCE, COURAGE, STRENGTH, AND SUCCESS	Cinnamon, Holly, Patchouli, Thistle, Yarrow
WISDOM	Sage
PROTECTION	Basil, Comfrey, Holly, Hyssop, Pennyroyal, Rue

CRYSTALS	OILS
Jet, Obsidian, Onyx	Camphor, Juniper, Mugwort, Patchouli
Emerald, Smoky Quartz, Blue Topaz	Lavender, Jasmine
Amethyst, Clear Quartz, Selenite	Cedar, Eucalyptus, Lemon, Peppermint, Tea Tree
Selenite, Turquoise	Frankincense, Rose, Sandalwood
Amethyst, Moonstone, Obsidian, Rose Quartz	Bergamot, Chamomile, Rosemary, Ylang Ylang
Agate, Amethyst, Hematite, Jasper, Clear Quartz, Shiva Lingam, Tiger's Eye	Catnip, Chamomile, Myrrh, Oregano, Tea Tree, Valerian
Amethyst, Moonstone, Obsidian, Clear Quartz	Frankincense, Jasmine, Rose, Sandalwood
Amber, Onyx, Tiger's Eye, Yellow Topaz	Cedar, Cinnamon, Lemon, Orange
Moonstone, Turquoise	Cedar, Neroli
Amber, Carnelian, Hematite, Jet, Onyx	Basil, Frankincense, Juniper, Pennyroyal, Vetiver

Essential Oils

Many people practicing witchcraft today use essential oils in their magic. Extracted from herbs, essential oils contain the magical properties of the plant from which they're drawn. Essential oils should never be applied directly to the skin, as that can cause irritation. Instead, dilute them in a base oil—an unscented oil like jojoba or grapeseed.

You can use a single oil in your work, or combine essential oils based on your magical purpose. If you can't find the essential oil combination you want at the store, you can also blend your own oils. Start with ⅛ cup of your base oil. Add a few drops of each essential oil you want to work with, such as lavender, eucalyptus, or tea tree. Swirl the cup to blend.

In addition, if you are pregnant or nursing, consult with a health-care professional before working with essential oils.

Though spells might specify a particular herb, crystal or oil, you can generally substitute another herb, stone, or oil that has the same properties. Use the chart on the previous pages to find out what substitutions you can make.

Auras and Colors

An aura is a luminous energy field that surrounds all living beings. Although auras haven't been scientifically proven, there's a theory that auras have colors. You can learn a lot about a person by the color of their aura. Because your aura represents how you feel emotionally and physically, if you're able to see another person's aura, it can give you an idea of who their true self is; likewise, your own aura reflects how you're feeling to others. Most people can see auras with a bit of practice—to see yours, place your hand, palm down and fingers slightly separated, on a piece of white paper. Look at your hand, in the areas between your fingers, and let your eyes go slightly out of focus. You'll begin to see a soft glow around your hand. What color is it? That's your aura shining through.

Interpretations vary, but traditionally, a pure white aura is a sign of someone who is spiritually enlightened, while a black one indicates a person with a profound sense of unhappiness. Red auras represent confidence and passion, and orange is the color of artists and creative people. If someone's aura is green, they often are a healer and helper, and a blue aura signifies a person who's intuitive and sensitive. People deeply connected to nature and the outdoors often have a brown, earthy aura. Auras can change colors, based upon how you feel physically, emotionally, and spiritually.

Divination, Tarot, and Pendulums

Divination is the act of seeking knowledge of things to come via metaphysical or supernatural means. A few methods in particular are popular among today's witchcraft practitioners. Most people find that they prefer one or two over the others, and that's fine—you don't have to master every single one.

Tarot cards are one of the most popular forms, and although it may seem like the cards "predict the future," most readers will tell you that they simply offer guidance based upon the current situation. Tarot is a tool for self-awareness and lends itself well to inner healing.

Pendulum divination is an easy method to learn—simply ask yes/no questions while dangling a pendulum, and see which way it swings. You can purchase a pendulum commercially or make your own. Most people use a crystal or stone, but any weighted object will do—just attach it to the end of a string or chain. There are many ways to use a pendulum for divination; you'd be amazed what you can learn if you ask the right questions.

Another popular form of divination includes casting runes, which are carved or painted stones from the Norse tradition. Each has a symbol on it, and the reader interprets the symbols in the context of the question being asked. You can also read tea leaves; drink a cup of tea and leave a few of the loose leaves in the bottom. By looking for patterns, you can find solutions to the issue at hand.

Charms, Talismans, and Amulets

A magical charm, sometimes called a talisman or amulet, is a great tool for healing. A charm is used to attract good fortune, prosperity, or healing, while an amulet often provides protection, either from harm or illness. A talisman is an item that can be enchanted with specific properties of your choosing—healing, love, luck, or abundance. Throughout history, people have carried these for protection and healing magic.

Making your own charm is very simple. Sacred items like stones or dried herbs can be placed in a pouch and carried or worn, or you can consecrate a piece of special jewelry as a healing charm. You may want to use a natural item such as a stone with a hole in it, or a piece of wood or bone.

Altars

The altar is a place where you can perform rituals and spellwork. For many witches, the altar is the heart of their magical practice. Ideally, set your altar up in an area where you can leave it in place permanently. It's easy to make an altar out of any flat surface. Do you have a table, cabinet, or bookcase that's not being used? Convert it into an altar.

With a permanent altar, you can change the décor to reflect the seasons, moon phases, or specific magical purposes. Consider themed altars if you've got the space; in addition to my permanent altar, where I do the bulk of my magical work, I also have an ancestor shrine, a healing altar on a pretty shelf over my claw-footed bathtub, a prosperity altar above my desk, and a nature altar for found items like shells, stones, bones, and branches. Figure out what sort of altar space works best for you personally, and design one that brings joy to your spirit.

SETTING UP YOUR ALTAR

The altar is the focus of ritual and spellwork for modern witches, and you can put anything you like on yours. You might want to include the following items, so that you can make sure you've got everything you need at your fingertips before you start your magical work:

- Symbols of the four elements: earth, air, fire, and water. You can use a dish of clean soil for earth, a feather or fan to represent air, a simple tealight candle to symbolize fire, and a cup or bowl of fresh water.
- Candles
- Incense
- A magic wand or other tools used to direct energy
- Your grimoire or Book of Shadows (notebook of spells and magical ideas)
- Spell or ritual components

Organize your altar items in a way that makes them easy to reach during your magical work. You may even want to add a photo or sketch to your grimoire, so you can easily reassemble your altar the next time you want to work with it.

Use a Journal or Grimoire to Track Your Journey

One of the most valuable tools a witch can have is a dedicated place to write down spells, rituals, and other ideas. You can call it a grimoire, your Book of Shadows or simply your journal. Some people believe a grimoire should be handwritten; this transfers energy to the writer and helps you memorize the contents efficiently.

If you find a ritual or spell somewhere else that you like and want to work with, be sure to note the source in your grimoire. Keeping track of where you got the spell and who wrote it will help you keep things straight on your magical journey, and you'll start to recognize patterns in the works of other practitioners. With each spell or ritual you perform, write down the results and outcome—or lack thereof. The more you keep track of, the better you'll be able to fix your mistakes in the future. Perhaps most important, keeping a written record of your work will allow you to look back in years to come, to see how far you've traveled since your first step.

Grimoire Best Practices

If you're ready to set up your magical grimoire or Book of Shadows, there are a lot of things you can include. Here are a few things you might want to write in your magical journal:

- A dedication, including your name and the date you started your grimoire
- Gods and goddesses of your particular belief system
- The uses and qualities of various herbs (herbal correspondences)
- The uses and qualities of various crystals (crystal correspondences)
- Sabbats and other celebrations you might want to observe throughout the year
- Moon phases and their meanings
- Divination methods, such as Tarot, pendulums, runes, or reading tea leaves
- Spells and rituals that you've performed or plan to perform
- Sacred texts and a list of relevant reading material

Treat your grimoire as a sacred object and keep it near your altar for easy access.

Cleansing Your Space

If you work best when your space is neat and tidy, you're going to love this part. It's a good idea to cleanse your sacred space before performing any magical work. This doesn't just mean physically cleaning it—although that's also valuable, since it's hard to focus on effective magic when there's dust and candle wax all over your altar. But here, cleansing means spiritual cleanup—eliminating negative energy before you begin working your magic.

There are a number of different effective cleansing methods, so choose the one that resonates best with you. Some people like to burn purifying herbs—in many traditions, this is referred to as smudging. It's a custom that goes back thousands of years, operating on the theory that the smoke carries negativity away into the universe. You can light sage, juniper, cedar, or other dried herbs and walk in a clockwise direction, wafting any bad vibes up into the smoke and out of your space.

Other traditions use a method called asperging, which is the use of liquid to purify an area. You can use wine, milk blended with honey, or water that's been left out to charge overnight under a full moon or in bright sunlight for a day. Place your consecrated liquid in a bowl or cup and dip the tips of your fingers in it. Lightly sprinkle it around your sacred space as you walk in a clockwise direction. See the sidebar on page 12 for more ideas.

Casting and Closing a Circle

The purpose of casting a circle is to designate an area as sacred; it keeps the good energy in and the negative energy out. You can cast a circle anywhere you like—indoors or outdoors—and your circle can be any size. Although you don't have to cast a circle every time you do a spell or ritual, many practitioners find that it gets them in the right mindset for magic.

To cast a circle, imagine a circle surrounding your work area and figure out which direction you wish to face when you start—some traditions call for north, others east, but it's entirely up to you. This method starts in the east, but you can adapt it as needed; there's no one right way to cast a circle.

Begin on the east side of your space, face the outside of your circle. Raise your hands—or wand—to the sky and say, "Guardians of the east, powers of air, I call upon you to watch over this sacred space." Feel free to embellish your invocation as much as you like, and then slowly walk in a clockwise direction until you're facing south. Say, "Guardians of the south, powers of fire, I call upon you to watch over this sacred space." Repeat this in the west, calling upon water guardians, and in the north, invoking the powers of the earth. Once you've gone all the way around, your circle is cast.

To close, or dismiss, the circle at the end of your magical work session, repeat the process backward. Start with whichever direction you ended at in your original circle casting. Facing outside your circle, say, "Guardians of the north, powers of the earth, I thank you for protecting this sacred space." Work your way around counterclockwise until you reach your original starting point. Once you get there, your circle is uncast.

Incense and Candles

After you light incense, the smoke will carry your intentions out into the universe. Incense is available in sticks, cones, and loose-leaf blends. For a stick or cone, simply light the end and let it burn. For loose incense, light a charcoal disc—available in most metaphysical shops—and after it's hot, add a thin layer of loose incense on top of it. You'll see your incense gradually begin to burn.

Candles work along the same principle. It's a good idea to have a selection of candles in various shapes and colors for spellwork. Use red for courage and love, pink for friendship and emotions, and orange for attraction and encouragement. If you need financial bounty, pick up some green or gold candles. For healing magic, use light blue for overall health, patience, and understanding; and dark blue for anxiety and vulnerability. If you don't have colored candles, a white one is always an acceptable substitute for just about any purpose. A burning candle illuminates your intention, and—as with incense—carries that intention out into the heavens to help you manifest your goal.

Wands

While magic wands might sound cliché, they do come into play in many magical belief systems. The wand is used to direct energy—energy that you've drawn in and energy that you're putting out into the universe. Although the wand can be made of any material you like, it's traditionally crafted from wood.

To make your own wand, go for a walk outdoors. Look at the ground to see what branches might be lying there waiting for you—but don't harvest a live branch from a tree. When you find one you feel drawn to, pick it up and hold it. Does it feel comfortable in your hand? Do you like its energy? If so, that's the one for you. When you take it home, you may want to remove the bark and sand it, or you might choose to leave it as it. If you strip the bark, polish the branch with oil to protect it and keep it from drying out.

Different woods have various magical associations; you can select one based on these correspondences. For instance, an oak branch symbolizes power, while willow and rowan are associated with protection. For prophecy and divination, consider alder wood; make a wand of hawthorn for magic related to business decisions. Cherry, maple, and Osage orange are all related to healing magic.

Mortar and Pestle

If you're doing spellwork or rituals that involve herbs or other dried organic material, it's useful to get a mortar and pestle. This grinding and crushing implement has been around for thousands of years and consists of two parts; the mortar is typically a bowl or flat surface, and the pestle is club-shaped, with blunt ends, and held in the hand. Although the mortar and pestle set is primarily used for food production, it became popular in fifteenth-century Europe as a tool to grind medicinal plants and resins.

When you use a mortar and pestle, place the dried herbs in the bowl and hold it steady with one hand. With the other hand, hold the pestle, pressing it down into the mortar, moving it back and forth or in a circle. This will grind the herbs down as finely as you want—even into powders—for use in spellwork. If you also use a mortar and pestle for food preparation, get a second, dedicated one for magical workings—you don't want to use the same mortar and pestle for both.

The Magical Broom

The witch's broom is so iconic that it's almost a stereotype—witches in almost every film, TV show, and children's picture book are depicted toting brooms as they go about their magical business. The magical broom, called a "besom" in some traditions, is associated with purification and cleansing, and is used for clearing out negative energies from a ceremonial area. Since most people have a broom in their homes, it's easy to keep one standing unobtrusively in the corner, and your guests are unlikely to question it. If you use a broom for cleaning, make sure to get a second, dedicated one for magic—again, you don't want to use your magical objects to cook, clean, or perform other mundane duties.

To use your broom for magical work, start at an open door, and sweep around each room in a counterclockwise direction to banish negative energy out the door. You can also use it to welcome in abundance, love, and other positive things by sweeping clockwise. In some traditions, laying a broomstick across the threshold ensures that only visitors with good intentions will enter.

Tools around Your Home

There are other items you may find useful to have on hand for magical work. Invest in some parchment or nice paper—you'll find many spells involve writing down your intention—as well as a good pen. You'll also want some jars and bottles to use for spellwork involving container magic. Use scrap fabric for magical pillows, sachets, or charm bags. Finally, make sure you have a bowl to blend your magical herbs in; the most effective ones are made of natural materials such as wood or clay. You can also use one made of ceramic, which is a product of naturally occurring raw materials.

How Often Should You Practice Magic?

When you finally discover the power of effective spellwork, you're probably going to be tempted to work magic all the time, for just about everything. But this can get overwhelming fast. In general, it's a good idea to avoid casting too many similar spells within the same 24-hour period. For example, you might wish to work a healing ritual and a community-building spell the same evening, but don't do two healing spells for the same person at the same time. Witchcraft does require focus and effort, and if you're working on numerous spells with similar focus at the same time, you'll likely find that your attention and energy are spread too thin.

Different spells also tend to work at different speeds. A healing working might manifest more quickly than one that brings long-term prosperity into your home. Spells don't always have immediately visible outcomes—so don't obsess about your results day in and day out. Learn to be patient and look for small signs that your spell is creating change.

Some spells are designed to be worked on over a designated period of time. For instance, the Decluttering Ritual (page 145) is specifically meant to take place for 13 days. The results should appear within that time frame, so don't repeat the working until you know your allotted number of days or weeks have passed. In other cases, spells are formulated to be repeated regularly, such as the Nature Meditation spell (page 68) and the Spell to Heal the Environment (page 122).

A grimoire or Book of Shadows is the best way to keep track of how effective your timing is. If you find that you're getting results quickly, great! If you haven't seen anything begin to manifest within 28 days—a full lunar cycle—it may be time to reevaluate your work and then try again.

Let's Start Healing

The information you've just read is a very bare-bones summary of magical practice, but it will help you get started. Remember, you don't have to be an experienced witch to perform healing spells and rituals, but having a basic understanding of magical tools, techniques, and principles will help. If you'd like to learn more in-depth information about modern witchcraft, be sure to check the list of recommended books in the Resources section at the end of this book.

Conclusion

We've covered some of the basics of modern magical practice, including what hands-on tools to use. However, witchcraft is more than just tools and physical trappings. It's also a mental practice. And if we're going to do some full-contact healing, we'll need to get into the right mindset for effective spellwork. In the next chapter, we'll discuss how to calm your mind so you can cast spells and perform rituals with confidence.

We'll learn how to approach healing our own negative thoughts, as well as ways to manage anxiety and stress, and boost self-esteem, all while setting magical intentions. With the 10 spells in the next chapter, you'll be able to embark on the radical, subversive act of healing your mind, and manifesting a powerful, healthy new life for yourself.

Calm Your Mind

One of the most powerful implements in your magical arsenal is your own mind. By calming your mind, you can develop an outlook that allows you to focus your efforts and energy on your magical goals, thus making your practice more successful. In this chapter, we'll learn how to move away from the negative thoughts that are affecting our lives and toward healing. We'll talk about a few magical self-esteem boosters, methods of silencing the inner critic, and ways to manage your anxiety and stress. In addition, we'll discuss how to set goals and magical intentions, and manifest the life you want. You'll get a chance to try 10 spells, remedies, and rituals all aimed at helping calm your mind and make you feel empowered.

The Power of a Peaceful Mind

There's a lot to be said for a mind that's clear of clutter, anxiety, and frustration. You probably spend many of your waking hours preoccupied by things you need to do, people who have upset you, hurt feelings you can't just ignore, worries about jobs and money, or past trauma that bogs you down. We all do. But when we give ourselves permission to relax and clear it all out, our minds slow down a bit, and they open up to potential and possibility. Suddenly, there's room in there for new ideas, creativity, joy, love, and optimism. Inner turmoil in the mind creates clamor, while an empty space welcomes peace. When you develop the ability to achieve peacefulness, you can act from that mindset, and have a positive impact on the world around you.

How Witchcraft Can Help

A witch is someone who honors the divine in themselves as they seek out peace and truth, and thus is able to serve as their own healer. That's pretty empowering—the idea that witchcraft can heal the self. Witches can use transformative magic to find balance, discover our authentic selves, and shift negative, destructive thoughts and behaviors into powerful, positive ones.

Witchcraft can be therapeutic, in that it allows us to step away from feelings of guilt and shame, and instead embrace our genuine selves. In her groundbreaking book *Daring Greatly,* Brené Brown says, "Let go of who you think you're supposed to be; embrace who you are." Transformative, self-focused witchcraft will lead you to do just that.

But how, exactly, can you do this with witchcraft? Well, you can use witchcraft to:

Heal Your Thoughts

By practicing magic focused on radical self-care, you can eliminate emotional patterns that cause you to feel as though you're somehow *less than*. Self-care spells are a powerful way to remind yourself that you matter, you're strong, and you are worthy of being treated with respect and love.

Soothe Your Inner Critic

Are you your own worst critic? How many times have you told yourself that you're not enough or too much? That you're too fat or too thin? That you work too much or not enough? With empowering rituals and spellwork, you can silence that nagging little voice, and replace it with one that tells you what an amazing person you are, and what an even more amazing person you're about to become. That inner critic has no place in your head if you don't allow it to stay.

Manage Anxiety and Stress

It's easy to get anxious and stressed out—you've got family and work to tend to, you might be concerned about finances or housing, or perhaps you're just overwhelmed by life in general. Focused rituals and meditations can help you manage these feelings.

That's not to say that witchcraft is a substitute for professional mental health treatment. If you suffer from depression, anxiety, or another mental health condition, make sure to consult a medical professional for treatment. However, using witchcraft in tandem with therapy, medication, or other treatment can help ease your way toward a healthier mindset.

Boost Your Self-Esteem

There's a sense of empowerment that comes with practicing witchcraft, and that is largely because it allows us to feel like we have control over something in our lives. You might not be able to control your cranky coworker, your misbehaving kids, or that astronomically high utility bill that just came in, but you *can* control the way you respond to these things. Magical self-care puts the ball back into your court. Once you've got control over a situation, it's a little easier to feel confident. And the more confident you feel, the more effective your magic will be, full circle. As you become more self-assured in your magical practice, that will spill over into your non-magical life, and you'll discover that you're pretty darn great after all.

Get Clear on Your Dreams and Desires

One of the keys to effective and successful magical practice is the ability to set goals. After all, if you don't know what you want, it's pretty hard to work toward it. Witchcraft forces you to evaluate what your true desires are. Establishing your dreams and desires will allow you to focus on the end results of your actions, both magical and mundane.

Set Intentions (and Commit to Them)

Witchcraft isn't for the faint of heart. You've got to make a commitment to doing the work. Any kind of transformation, whether it's magical or otherwise, begins with a declaration of intent. But anyone can say, "I want X to happen." People do it all the time. It's the actual work, the process that creates change, that can be a struggle. As you delve deeper into your magical practice, you'll learn how to set your intentions and then follow through—a practice that will also benefit you in the personal and professional parts of your mundane life.

Manifest the Life You Desire

There's an old saying: "To do magic is to express your desire to bring about change in things that dissatisfy you." What displeases you about your life? What do you want to change? So much of it is possible, when you set your intentions to manifest the life you want—but the first step is making the decision to change. Once you do so, the potential is limitless. Why not work to get what you want, in a way that brings about healing, peace, and power?

Spells, Remedies, and Rituals

Are you ready to start working toward magically calming your mind? These 10 spells, rituals, and basic remedies for self-care will form the foundation of your work to move forward in healing. With these simple actions, you'll be able to calm your mind and take the beginning steps in the direction of a new, positive, empowered life.

Morning Empowerment Affirmations

Every morning brings promise—the potential of starting fresh and anew. Why not start every day with an affirmation? It's a great way to set an intention to feel how you choose to feel, long before anyone else tells you otherwise.

STEPS:

To create an affirmation, choose statements that resonate for you; that's the best way to bring about positive change. Present-tense statements are far more powerful than predictive ones; instead of saying "I want" or "I will," use "I have" or "I am." Try one—or more—of these each morning, and repeat it three times:

- Gratitude: "I am thankful," or "I am blessed." Be sure to include what you're thankful for, whether it's a person, a situation, or just being alive.

- Love: "I choose to give and receive love," or "I have an open heart," or "I am compassionate and patient with others."

- Self-acceptance: "I am enough," or "I am more than the opinions others hold of me," or "I am worthy of joy and happiness."

- Forgiveness: "I am willing to change my point of view," or "I attempt to see the good in others," or "I am learning to forgive others and myself for the past."

Affirmations can be done anywhere, anytime, with no prep involved—you may want to light a candle to focus, but it's not necessary. All you need to do this is your own self.

As you say the words each morning, feel the meanings, and visualize how they can change your mindset. Consider how you'll adapt that affirmative phrase to the things you're going to do today. Repeat your affirmation throughout the day, because the more you remind yourself of it, the more your subconscious mind will seek out opportunities to boost that affirmation for you.

SELF-CARE VISION BOARD

Have you ever made a vision board? They're not just used in witchcraft; you may have created one as part of other spiritual or healing work. A vision board is simply a collection of images and words that serve as a reminder of what you hope to achieve in your self-care journey, and why it's important to you. Regularly seeing these motivating words and pictures will help your mind become more aware of your intentions, and guide you toward the destination.

MATERIALS:

A white candle
Cardstock or poster board, glue sticks, and scissors
Images from magazines or websites
Paper and pen, or printed text with words that inspire you

STEPS:

1. Light the candle. As you focus on the flame, visualize the goals you want to achieve.

2. Using these goals as a framework, find images that reflect the experiences and feelings you want to attract, and cut/print them out. Arrange them on the poster board. Do so thoughtfully; focus on visuals that inspire positive emotions.

3. Add words of affirmation. You can either handwrite them on paper, or you can print them out from your computer. You can use single words like "joy," "abundance," or "empowered," or select entire quotes that motivate you. Arrange them around the images so you can see them clearly.

4. Glue everything in place.

5. Say: "I call these things into my life, bringing me closer to my goals. I will these things to happen in my life, bringing me closer to my dreams. I draw these things into my life, making my visions reality."

6. Hang your vision board in a place of prominence in your home. Look at it several times each day. Contemplate the things displayed on your board. Before you go to bed at night, spend time visualizing your goals, affirming them, and considering how you'll bring your visions to fruition.

TIME MANAGEMENT MAGIC

Everyone's got the same 24 hours in our day—so why does it seem like some people get a whole lot more done? Are they slowing down time? No, but they're managing their hours effectively. With a bit of time management magic, you can gain better control over your own time. Do this working on a Saturday, which is associated with the god Saturn—Father Time.

MATERIALS:

A yellow candle, associated with self-worth and personal power
A windup watch with hands

STEPS:

1. Light the candle. As you focus on the flame, think about how you're currently using your time, and determine where you need a few extra hours in your day.

2. Hold the watch in your hands, and close your eyes. Think about the things you'll do if you have more time available.

3. Say: "Time has value, so they say, I'll accomplish so much, every day. I charge this watch, by Saturn's power, giving me extra minutes and hours."

4. Wear or carry the watch, and keep it wound. When you feel like you're running low on time, hold it in your hands once more, and refocus your efforts toward getting things done.

Setting Protective Boundaries

Everyone gets excited when you say "yes" to doing something they asked you to. But you probably worry about the consequences of saying no. How will others view you if you refuse? Will people think you're uncooperative, selfish, or mean? Here's a secret: "No" is one of the most powerful words in the English language, because it's a source of power. "No" is not the same thing as negativity. Instead, it's a moment of clear choice that makes a declarative statement. Which is why learning to say "no" is a magical act of self-preservation. "No, I can't help with your project. No, thank you. No, I'm not able to give you money." These statements take a stand and say that although you value your interactions with others, you aren't going to let yourself be manipulated or influenced by them.

RAGE RELEASE

When you're angry, it's probably hard to shed those furious feelings and calm your mind. Maybe you've been wronged, or you're upset about something beyond your control, or something hurtful that someone did or said. Regardless, keeping rage bottled up is unhealthy, because it can color your perspective of the world around you. Channel your hostility into energy and get rid of it.

MATERIALS:

A pot of loose soil
A shovel

STEPS:

1. Keep the pot of soil outside, in a place that's easily accessible.

2. When you're angry, go outside and sit next to your pot of soil. Close your eyes, and imagine your rage and anger flowing from your mind down through your arms and into your hands. Rub your hands together, forming the rage into a ball of energy.

3. Plunge your fingers into the soil, as deep as you can go, and visualize that ball of rage burrowing into the dirt. Move the soil around to cover the rage, pushing it far down beneath the surface.

4. Say: "Rage and anger, I banish you. Rage and anger, I dismiss you. Rage and anger, I bury you."

5. When you're done, take your pot of soil somewhere away from your home, dig a hole, and dump the soil in it. Cover it up and go home without looking back.

Spiritual Spring Cleaning

This is a method of decluttering your brain. By shedding what you don't need, you can make room for the things you do need. Banish the negative, welcome in the positive.

MATERIALS:

A blue candle (blue is associated with healing)
Paper and pen
A fireproof dish

STEPS:

1. Light the blue candle and sit quietly for a moment, meditating on the flame and visualizing your healing goals.

2. Draw a line to make two columns on the paper. In the first, list feelings or emotions that you'd like to eliminate. Write each down individually, like "anxiety," "fear," "judgment," or "poor self-image."

3. In the second column, write the opposite of each negative feeling. For example, you might put "confidence" across from "fear," or write "pride" across from "shame."

4. Tear the paper in half down the center, so you have two separate lists. Take your negative list and tear it into tiny pieces. Drop the pieces into the dish and set them on fire.

5. As the pieces burn, say: "I have no room for negativity. I burn away what doesn't serve me."

6. Once the fire has burned out, dispose of the ashes in running water.

7. Take the second piece of paper, with your positive thoughts, and fold it up. Carry it in your pocket. Whenever you're not sure what you want to attract, open it up and re-read it as a refresher.

PRAYER BEADS FOR REFLECTION

Prayer beads are a powerful meditative tool found in many religions. You can create a set of your own that highlights your goals, affirmations, and intentions, giving you a focal point for meditation and reflection.

MATERIALS:

Beads in your favorite colors, sizes, and shapes, in natural materials
Beading wire or string

STEPS:

1. Sort your beads and assign them different meanings based on colors, sizes, and shapes. For instance, blue could indicate hopes, while purple connotes goals; large beads could symbolize behavioral changes you intend to make. Select a few to represent the positive affirmations that you're making.

2. Arrange them in a pattern you like. Try different layouts to see what makes the most sense and resonates the most with you.

3. Once you determine your layout, string them on the beading wire and knot it securely.

4. Consecrate your beads by holding them in your hands. Visualize your magical energy flowing through them, and say: "I bless these beads with my personal power, I bless these beads with positive vibrations, I bless these beads for the higher good."

5. To use your prayer beads, hold them in your hands when you meditate. Go through the strand, one bead at a time, reflecting on the meanings, intentions, and affirmations of each one. Do this daily, to reinforce your self-healing goals and practices. If your bead strand is long enough, you may even wish to wear it like a necklace, so those reminders will always be with you.

CENTER YOURSELF

In many magical traditions, centering is the cornerstone of energy work. Although various forms of witchcraft utilize different approaches to centering, this method is an easy meditative exercise that will help you create a foundation for future magical thought and practice.

STEPS:

1. Find a place where you can work undisturbed and sit comfortably. Turn off the phone and lock the door if you have to.

2. Begin by closing your eyes and taking a long, deep breath. Hold it for a moment, and then exhale slowly. Repeat this a few times, until your breath is even, calm, and regular.

3. Bring the palms of your hands close together, keeping them about an inch apart. Move them around, as though you were trying to warm them, but maintaining the gap between them.

4. You should eventually begin feeling a tingling between your hands; this is energy. If you don't feel it the first time you do this, keep trying. Focus on that tingling space, and visualize the energy there pulsating, contracting, and expanding.

5. Imagine that energy spreading around your entire body, and then draw it inward so that it's centered.

Each time you do this, you'll repeat the process of regulating your breathing and then harnessing your own energy. When you perform spellwork and rituals, draw on this energy to manifest your goals.

BATHTUB MAGIC

Even though true self-care involves a lot more than just soaking in a tub, there's a lot to be said for the quiet, meditative relaxation of a bath. It's a great way to unwind and rejuvenate your system. If you're worried it might seem too indulgent, a 2018 study by Yasuaki Goto and Shinya Hayaska determined that people who immersed their bodies in warm water at least once a week saw improvements in their physical and emotional health.

MATERIALS:

A bathtub
2 cups Epsom salts
10 drops lavender essential oil
5 drops rose essential oil
A white candle, associated with healing emotions and cleansing the mind
Optional: a cup of your favorite herbal tea, reading material, relaxing music

STEPS:

1. Fill your tub with warm water, then add the Epsom salts and the essential oils.

2. Light the candle and climb into the tub.

3. Close your eyes and breathe deeply, inhaling the soft scent of lavender. Feel the warm water on your skin. Allow yourself to become immersed, and picture yourself floating weightless, free of stress, anxiety, or trouble.

4. Open your eyes and focus on the candle, keeping your breathing regular. As you watch the flame, wash your body and visualize all of your worries being scrubbed away.

5. Once your skin is clean, you can read, drink tea, or listen to music, if you'd like.

6. When the water cools, climb out of the tub, and unplug the bath. Your apprehension and discontent will go down the drain.

LEARN TO
FORGIVE YOURSELF

Guilt is something most of us carry with us. It's hard to eliminate, because when we do or say something wrong, we often don't just think about the action. We generalize toward ourselves based on that action, and decide that we're bad people.

Learning to forgive yourself can help increase your sense of self-worth. Try exploring these ideas, in a journal or in your interactions with others:

- Allow yourself self-compassion and accept that doing a bad thing doesn't make you a bad person.
- Don't magnify things out of proportion. Are your feelings of guilt appropriate to the level of the offense you caused?
- If you've hurt someone else, apologize—not for what you believe you did, but for what they believe you did.
- Ask yourself what you can learn from the experience, and then focus on the lesson, rather than the mistake.

Little Charm Bag of Inspiration

Charm bags are a popular magical talisman in many traditions and belief systems. A charm bag is a portable method of carrying a spell with you at all times, and it's a great way to work magic that is ongoing. To make a charm bag, you can sew a small drawstring pouch from the fabric of your choice, or you can simply cut a square of cloth and tie it closed. If possible, do this spell at the time of the full moon, which is associated with inspiration and wisdom.

MATERIALS:

A light blue drawstring bag, or a square of light blue fabric
Pinch dried sage
Bay leaf
A small piece of frankincense resin
A small piece of moonstone

STEPS:

1. Place the herbs, frankincense, and moonstone in the bag and close it.

2. Hold the bag between your palms and envision the inspiration you wish to receive. Speak your intention out loud: "I open myself up to creative ideas," or "I will make educated choices." Focus the energy of your intention into the bag.

3. Carry the charm bag with you, either in a pocket or worn around your neck as an amulet, to attract inspiration and wisdom into your life. When you need a reminder of its purpose, hold it in your hands once more, and focus on your intentions.

NATURE MEDITATION

One of the best things you can do to calm your mind is spend time outdoors. Whether you're able to walk in a large tree-filled park, or simply sit on your balcony and look at the clouds, the natural world can soothe even the most restless spirit. To do this simple meditation, go outside on a sunny day—you don't need any tools or supplies—and let your subconscious guide you.

STEPS:

1. Find a place where you can sit undisturbed and connect with all of the aspects of nature around you. Try to sit so that as much of your body as possible is in direct contact with the ground, a tree, or other natural elements.

2. Relax your body, close your eyes, and breathe deeply. Allow your senses to attune to nature. Listen to the sounds, smell the fragrant air, feel the breeze on your skin.

3. Turn your face toward the sun. Feel its warmth coursing over you, spreading down your body gradually, and eventually connecting you to the earth beneath you.

4. Feel your connection to the earth, and imagine yourself growing roots, extending deep into the soil, creating stability and strength. Keep your breathing deep and regular, and allow yourself to become one with the soil, the grass, and the seeds and rocks beneath the surface.

5. Say: "I am part of nature, nature is part of me. I embrace all of the gifts the natural world has to offer me. I am grounded in the spirit of the earth, and free in the spirit of the sky."

6. When you feel yourself becoming restless, slowly open your eyes, and express your gratitude to both the earth and the sky. Leave a token of thanks at the place where you sat, such as freshly picked flowers, a pretty stone, or a seashell.

Conclusion

Once you start focusing on calming your mind and integrating positive thought processes into your life, it becomes easier to start working on bringing about the changes you wish to manifest. With holistic and radical self-care, as the mind heals and becomes well, the body and spirit will follow.

In the next chapter, we'll look at the many ways magic and witchcraft can help make your physical body feel empowered and inspired. We'll explore some healthy eating and exercise concepts, the value of maintaining a positive body image, and how we can use magical practice to heal some of those pesky aches and pains. We'll get a chance to start working with spells, rituals, and activities that promote a healing body and an empowered physical self-image.

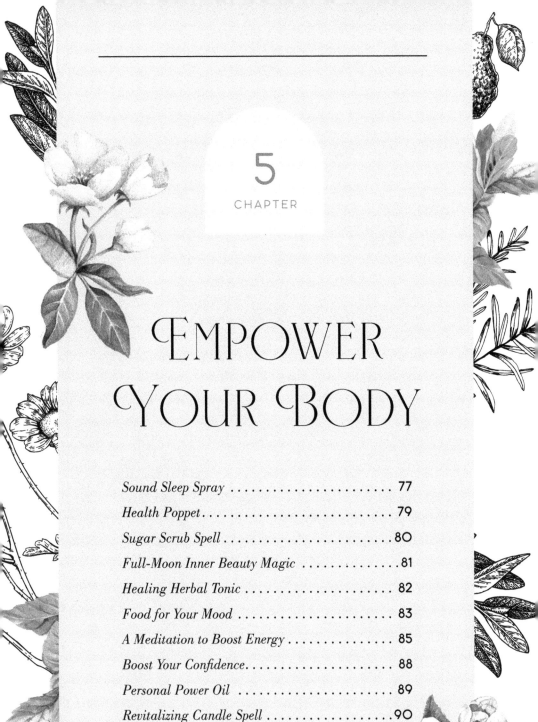

Empower Your Body

The ability to feel good all over is a holistic process. The mind, body, and spirit all have to work together and reinforce one another. When one is impacted, the rest follow suit. Radical self-care includes taking care of your physical self as well as your emotional and spiritual aspects. In this chapter, you'll learn ways that witch-craft can help your body, and how proper skin care, a nutritious diet, and physical activity can be beneficial to that holistic cycle. You'll learn rituals, spells, and other practices to help you feel better physically, from healing aches and pains to preventive measures like eating well and knowing your own limits.

Witchcraft and the Physical Body

The human body is a wondrous thing. From your fingers and toes to the synapses firing away in your brain, you're a unique machine—there's no other body quite like yours. When you activate your physical self and involve your witchcraft, the body becomes a magical vessel. How you care for it directly impacts who you are as a person—and this has nothing to do with the size or shape of your physical self.

It's about making deliberate choices in the way you treat yourself, allowing for a more successful magical practice. If you feel good physically, you'll feel more powerful in your magical workings. By taking advantage of simple practices like eating mindfully, getting enough rest, and engaging in regular movement, you'll build a physical self that can tackle any challenge.

Your Body Hears What Your Mind Says

A healthy body image starts in your mind, not a mirror. Do you truly accept the way you look and feel right now, or are you fixated on how society says you *should* look? The way you view your body isn't just about tolerating your appearance. Body positivity focuses on true acceptance of the person you are, and recognizing the qualities that make you feel strong, beautiful, and empowered despite any perceived imperfections. It relieves you of the pressure of a so-called "perfect body" as an aspirational goal.

Part of radical self-care is the ability to look at yourself and think, "Wow, I'm pretty great." If you're instead thinking, "Ugh, I hate the way my hips/ tummy/butt/skin/hair look," your body is going to respond accordingly. Love your body, and it will love you back.

Managing Constant Self-Criticism

If a healthy body image boosts our confidence, then the converse is true as well—constant self-criticism and doubt is an esteem-killer. Overcoming self-criticism is hard, particularly if you've had people in your life belittle you. This negative inner dialogue creates a barrier to achieving goals and dreams, because it subtly convinces you that you don't deserve joy. Because your thoughts can turn into self-fulfilling prophecies, if you tell yourself,

"I'll never be happy," or "I'm not good enough for this," you'll sabotage your chances of success without even knowing you're doing it.

Pay attention to your inner dialogue and look for patterns. Are there certain situations that trigger self-doubt? Find ways to distract yourself when self-criticism rears its ugly head; sometimes, the best way to conquer it is to do something you know you're good at. Make an effort to replace negative concepts with positive ones. For instance, if your brain is telling you, "I can't go to the gym, I have no idea how to use the equipment, and what if people make fun of me?" switch it out for "I can't wait to start feeling healthier again, and I'm excited to learn about lifting those kettlebells." Finally, ask yourself what you'd tell your best friend if they were constantly self-criticizing—then follow your own advice.

The Power of Speaking Kindly to Yourself

Develop a habit of challenging yourself when destructive self-talk pops up, and you can start building a kind and positive relationship with your own mind and body. Talk to yourself like you would anyone else who was feeling down. If your sibling or neighbor felt bad after not achieving a goal, would you call them a loser and a failure? Or would you be supportive and reassuring?

Find a mantra to recite when you experience unkind thoughts about yourself. It can be something as simple as, "This too shall pass, I am worthy," or "I deserve good things." Perhaps your mantra will command you to think better of yourself: "Stop that—I am happy, healthy, and whole." Take time each day to remind yourself you're good enough. Make a list of qualities that bring you pride and review them regularly: "I am strong, I'm a good parent, I work hard, I'm loyal." Replace your negative thoughts with positive ones, and you'll soon see a difference.

Be Grateful for What You Have

Gratitude is more than just saying thanks. It's the concept of mindfully recognizing the things that you have and that you are. Sure, everyone would like to do more, achieve more, be more—but those will come with time. For now, try expressing thankfulness for what is, instead of focusing on what isn't. In other words, prioritize *I have* over *I want*. You can express gratitude by writing a list, telling a trusted friend, or simply meditating on the things you are grateful for.

It's not just successful people who benefit from the attitude of gratitude. A 2017 study by Dr. Joel Wong of Indiana University revealed that even among people who struggled with mental health issues, daily expressions of thankfulness inspired feelings of wellness and joy. Gratitude has a lasting impact on our brains and can help kick toxic emotions to the curb.

Certainly, not everyone has unlimited resources, and some people experience very real scarcity of the most basic needs. But if you're privileged enough to have things to be thankful for, acknowledge them. These things don't have to be fancy, complex, or expensive—you could be grateful for the way your body lets you play with your kids in the park, or for a nourishing meal you cooked yourself.

Using Witchcraft to Heal Your Aches and Pains

The notion of using witchcraft and magic to heal physical pain is hardly a new one. For thousands of years, people have turned to magical practitioners for relief from their bodily ailments. In cultures around the world, the local witch is first and foremost a healer. In early modern Spain, the *saludadores* worked to cure disease and find its root causes. During Europe's Middle Ages, witches used herbalism to treat aches, pains, and even broken bones. Even in the ancient world, the Greeks referred to magical practice as *pharmakon*, involving the extensive use of herbal potions for pain management.

Today, you can still use witchcraft to ease physical symptoms. Magic should work in tandem with professional medical expertise. Don't rely on magic as the sole cure for what ails you; use it in ways that bring about healing energy. With practices like healing oils, sleep spells, beauty magic, and herbal teas, you can facilitate physical wellness by way of witchcraft.

Your Body Is Your Home

You've only got one body, and it's yours for the entire length of your visit here on earth, so it's important to take good care of it. There are a number of simple actions you can incorporate into your daily routine to maintain a healthy physical body.

First and foremost, live in a way that's healthy. Do your best to eat foods that are nutritious. While it's not always a practical option, cooking your meals from scratch is a good way to ensure you're getting the best nutrition possible.

Get plenty of rest and establish regular sleep patterns when you can. Move around a lot—try to stay active in whatever way fits your resources and abilities. Avoid indulging in unhealthy behaviors; quit smoking, and don't overdo your alcohol consumption. Make sure you practice good hygiene, which is important not just for your physical health, but because it will improve how you see yourself. Try to do something physical each day that's enjoyable: meditate, do yoga, or go for a walk.

Spells, Remedies, and Rituals

Let's get started with some spells, remedies, and daily practices that will help you heal your physical self. By listening to your body and taking good care of it, you'll develop a sense of balance and harmony, boosting your own magical abilities. Your body is a valuable asset in your magical practice, so give yourself a little tune-up when it's needed. The workings in this section will guide your body toward feeling whole and healthy.

Again, healing magic isn't a substitute for treatment from health-care professionals. Keep getting your annual checkups, and if you have a chronic condition, make sure you're getting medical help, too. Use healing magic as a companion tool to medical treatment.

Sound Sleep Spray

Everyone needs a good night's sleep. But many of us don't get enough rest, and stagger through our days cranky and on edge as a result. If that's you, brew up a blend of this sleep spray to spritz on your pillow before bedtime, to fall asleep naturally.

MATERIALS:

Glass spray bottle
1 cup water
12 drops lavender essential oil
12 drops bergamot essential oil
6 drops clary sage essential oil

STEPS:

1. Blend the water and the essential oils in the spray bottle, and swirl gently in a clockwise direction to mix.

2. Before bedtime, spray a bit on your pillow and sheets.

3. As you spray, say: "Restful sleep come to me, calming dreams in the night. Restful sleep envelop me, that I wake up feeling right."

Be sure to swirl your sleep spray before each use, so the oils will be effectively blended. If you begin to notice any skin irritation, wash your bedding and stop using your spray immediately.

GET SOME REST

Your body needs regular rest. To sleep restfully each night, try some of the following:

- Place a salt lamp in your bedroom— many people believe these absorb negative energy and can promote a good night's sleep.
- Before you go to bed, say an End of Day Affirmation [page 111].
- Add a bowl of crystals that are associated with sleep and dreaming to your nightstand: obsidian, agate, amethyst, labradorite, and jasper.
- Spritz your bedding and pillow with Sound Sleep Spray [page 77].
- Keep herbs like lavender, chamomile, and lemon balm under your bed to promote calming dreams.

HEALTH POPPET

A poppet, or magical doll, is one of the simplest ways to work witchcraft for your own—or someone else's—benefit. By crafting a doll to represent yourself, and stuffing it with herbs and a stone all associated with overall healing, you can enchant it to bring about wellness for your body and spirit.

MATERIALS:

Blue fabric—blue represents physical and emotional healing
Needle, thread, scissors, and natural stuffing material such as cotton
Pinch dried chamomile
Pinch dried comfrey
Pinch dried feverfew
A small amethyst stone
A snippet of your hair to use as a magical link between you and
    the poppet
A blue candle

STEPS:

1. Cut the fabric into two human-shaped pieces—gingerbread person patterns are a good guideline. Stitch the two pieces together, right sides facing each other, around the edges, leaving a small opening. As you do, visualize healing energy infusing your poppet.

2. Turn your poppet right side out and fill loosely with stuffing. Add the herbs and the amethyst, as well as the hair, and then stitch the poppet shut. If you like, draw a face or write your name on it.

3. Light the candle and hold the poppet in your hands. Say: "I name you [your name], and you are my health. Bring wellness to my body, mind, and spirit. Keep me safe, strong, and healthy; protect me from illness and ailments. As you thrive, so shall I."

4. Place your poppet in a place of prominence where you can see it each day. Whenever you walk by, thank it for keeping you healthy and sound.

Sugar Scrub Spell

Good skin care goes a long way toward making your body feel better. Make your own bath scrub to help slough off dead skin when you bathe. This also stimulates the production of collagen, which helps keep your skin firm, radiant, and healthy. Be sure not to over-exfoliate; two to three times a week is plenty for most people. Any more can leave your skin dry and irritated.

MATERIALS:

A glass bowl
1 cup granulated sugar
¼ cup coconut oil, melted and liquified
10 drops lemon essential oil
5 drops lavender essential oil
A small jar with a lid

STEPS:

1. Place the sugar in the bowl and pour the coconut oil over it—you can melt the oil by microwaving it for about 20 seconds or lightly heat it in a pot on the stove—and then mix together. If it seems too wet, add more sugar. If it's not wet enough, add a bit more oil.

2. Add the essential oils and blend your mixture thoroughly. Scoop your sugar scrub into a jar for storage; it will keep for about three weeks.

3. To use your scrub, start by taking a warm shower to soften your skin. Place a small amount of sugar scrub on your washcloth or a loofah sponge and massage it along your body in small circular motions.

4. As you scrub, visualize illnesses and pain being drawn away from your body. Say: "Lemon and lavender, healing my skin, healing my body, without and within."

5. Let the water rinse the sugar thoroughly from your body. As it goes down the drain, visualize any ailments going right along with it.

Full-Moon Inner Beauty Magic

When it comes to beauty magic, don't worry about focusing on unrealistic, unattainable beauty standards. True beauty is found within, and beauty magic relies on our ability to find the things inside ourselves that are beautiful—and then celebrate them. Do this working during the full moon.

MATERIALS:

A yellow candle—yellow is associated with joy and happiness
A small handheld mirror

STEPS:

1. Go outside under the moonlight and light the candle. Focus on the flame, and say: "I am beautiful inside and out, and I am happy to be who I am."

2. Hold the mirror so that you can see your reflection, angling it so the moonlight shines upon you. Say: "Sister moon, in all your splendor and glory, shine upon me this night, and may your beauty be reflected upon me. Let my inner beauty shine outward for others to see."

3. Look at the candle once more and repeat three times, "I see my beauty inside and out, and I am happy to be who I am." Close your eyes and feel the moon's energy above you.

4. Extinguish the candle. Hang the mirror somewhere you can see it daily. Whenever you pass by it, look at your reflection and say, "I am beautiful."

HEALING HERBAL TONIC

Ginger is well-known as an antioxidant and anti-inflammatory that can relieve nausea, colds, muscle pain, and other ailments. Honey is also full of healing agents, so blending them together can pack a wallop when it comes to wellness. The act of drinking tea also has a meditative aspect to it that's highly beneficial on a spiritual level.

MATERIALS:

4 cups water
A fresh ginger root, about 3 inches long, peeled and sliced
Local honey
A large lemon, cut into slices

STEPS:

1. Place the water in a pot on your stove and add the ginger root. Bring to a boil.

2. Reduce to a simmer and allow the ginger to steep for 10 minutes. Add the lemon slices and continue steeping for 5 more minutes.

3. Pour the tea into mugs to serve and add a bit of honey to sweeten the flavor. Say: "Ginger tea, full of energy, health and hardiness come to me. I care for my body, mind, and soul, with healing power, I make myself whole."

4. Sit quietly as you drink your tea, focusing on the healing energy coursing through your body with each sip.

FOOD FOR YOUR MOOD

There's a saying that you are what you eat. While that doesn't necessarily mean you're a cheeseburger or a pound of chocolate, it's definitely true that what you eat has an impact on how you feel. Eating in a way that's mindful can be magical. Consider selecting foods based on magical properties to align with your intent. To feel grounded and safe, eat root vegetables—like carrots, potatoes, or beans—or freshly baked breads and cakes. To attract love, incorporate fresh fruits, fish, ginger, rosemary, or vanilla into your meals. Prep dishes with apples, chocolate, honey, and saffron for overall happiness. When possible, eat in a way that's healthy, nutritious, and sustainable. If you can grow your own vegetables or buy ingredients from a local source, do so. For this ritual, prepare your favorite meal and enhance your kitchen witchery game.

MATERIALS:

Recipe and ingredients for your favorite comfort food

STEPS:

1. Prepare your meal as you normally would, but as you work, visualize your magical intention flowing into the food. To attract things to you, such as love, prosperity, or healing, stir your food in a clockwise direction. If you need to eliminate something, like debt or illness or anger, stir counterclockwise.

2. If your recipe requires herbs or spices, think about the magical properties associated with them. For instance, consider using basil for magic focused on calming, cinnamon for developing intuitive gifts, or sage for wisdom.

CONTINUED

FOOD FOR YOUR MOOD

3. Once your meal is ready, offer a blessing or prayer before you eat. It can be as simple as "I am thankful to have this food before me, and I honor the earth by eating with gratitude."

4. Acknowledge your specific magical purpose as you eat, slowly and mindfully. You can say: "I eat this bread with intent, knowing it will bring me calmness, security, and stability," or "This soup is made with love, and will bring me healing and wellness."

Note: You might wish to have a candle burning, in the appropriate magical color, as you prepare your meal (refer back to page 43 for candle colors and meanings). But if you do, be sure it's an unscented one; you don't want your food to smell or taste like candles!

A Meditation to Boost Energy

Meditation isn't just relaxing—in fact, a 2005 Harvard University study showed it can physically change your brain for the better. And you don't have to be sitting in a quiet room to do it. Moving meditations—meditating while you walk, dance, or otherwise move— are just as effective as seated ones. If you're looking to experience exercise and your physical body differently, or you're just someone who has trouble sitting still, try using this meditation to boost your energy as you exercise.

STEPS:

1. Before you begin moving, close your eyes and breathe deeply. Remind yourself of *why* you want to exercise in the first place. Do you want to become stronger and develop more physical endurance? Release stress?

2. Become aware of every muscle, and how they all work together to create the wonder that is your body. Visualize strength and wellness flowing through yourself.

3. Say: "I am strong, I am healthy, I am aware. My body, my mind, and my spirit are attuned."

4. Begin your exercise routine, and as you get into your zone, find a focal point for your attention. Perhaps it's the sound of your feet hitting the pavement, the up and down motion of an elliptical machine, or the sensation of sweat forming on your skin. Use this

CONTINUED

A MEDITATION TO BOOST ENERGY

focal point as an anchor, and if your mind wanders, direct yourself back to your focus.

5. As you're exercising, remind yourself of your purpose. Repeat your mantra regularly, and add any specific goals you have, such as "My legs are preparing for a 5K."

6. When you're finished, take some time to ground yourself, calming your heart rate and remaining aware of your muscles. Breathe deeply and remind yourself that you are strong and healthy, and your body, mind, and spirit are connected.

Personal Wellness Altar

If personal wellness is on your list of magical intentions, set up an altar to support your goals. Any flat surface can become a sacred space in your home to remind you of the wellness you wish to manifest. Begin with a simple cloth in a color or pattern that invites tranquility. Include photos of emotional or physical health objectives you're working toward, a list of constructive habits to develop, or even your Self-Care Vision Board (page 56). Add sacred symbols that bring to mind balance, harmony, and peace, as well as herbs, oils, or crystals with healing properties. Make a ritual of starting your day with positive affirmations at your altar, as you focus on your healing and wellness journey.

BOOST YOUR CONFIDENCE

Everyone has days where they feel insecure, but this talisman will help put a bit of pride in your stride. As you feel more secure, you'll project an image of confidence that others find inspiring.

MATERIALS:

A pink candle for confidence
A purple candle for power and respect
A tiger's eye stone, associated with courage
Some jeweler's wire and needle nose pliers
A cord or chain to wear around the neck

STEPS:

1. Light the candles and place the stone between them. Close your eyes and ask yourself how life might be different if you were more confident.

2. Hold the stone in your hand and visualize courage flowing between the candles into the stone.

3. Say: "I am brave and strong. My value is not determined by the opinions of others. I have power, and I embrace it."

4. Using the pliers, wrap the wire gently around the stone, leaving a loop at the top. As you do this, say, "I give myself this blessing from the heart. I have nothing to fear, and I am empowered."

5. Hang the stone on the chain or cord and wear it when you'll be in a situation that causes doubt. When your confidence wanes, hold the stone, and repeat: "I have nothing to fear, and I am empowered."

PERSONAL POWER OIL

Blend a batch of oil to boost your personal power and energy vibrations. You can mix this ahead of time, store it in a small bottle, and use it to anoint your skin whenever you want to feel stronger. The herbs in this oil are associated with personal empowerment, courage, self-confidence, and strength.

MATERIALS:

A small bowl for mixing
⅛ cup unscented oil, such as grapeseed or safflower
2 drops clove essential oil
4 drops cedarwood essential oil
2 drops basil essential oil
Pinch powdered cinnamon

STEPS:

1. Pour the unscented base oil into the bowl. Add the essential oils individually, swirling the bowl gently in a clockwise direction to blend after each one.

2. As you blend the oils, say: "Strength and power and vitality, boost my body's energy, fight against adversity."

3. Add the cinnamon, blending it in by swirling. Store your oil in a dark-colored glass bottle and label it with the contents and date.

4. Dab a small amount of the oil on your skin as needed, or on candles for spells involving power and strength.

REVITALIZING CANDLE SPELL

The older you get, the more likely your body is to experience weird and unexplained aches and pains. If your get-up-and-go has gotten up and left, use this simple candle spell to promote energetic wellness, using the color red for vitality.

MATERIALS:

A red candle
A piece of paper and a pen
A fire-safe bowl or cauldron

STEPS:

1. Light the red candle. Focus on the flame and envision the energy you'd like to feel in your body.

2. Draw a picture of yourself on the paper. It doesn't have to be a great work of art; all that matters is that you understand it. As you draw, highlight the parts of your body that are aching or ill by circling them or drawing arrows.

3. Fold the paper three times, and say: "Aches and pains, I send you away and replace you with energy, with vigor, with stamina."

4. Use the candle's flame to light the piece of paper and drop it in the bowl to burn.

5. As it burns, focus on the candle flame once more. Say: "I call renewal, I call rejuvenation, I call revitalization into my body and my life."

6. Once the paper has burned away, take the ashes somewhere far from your home and bury them.

Conclusion

The human body is a pretty fantastic thing. Treat yours well, and it'll be kind to you in return. The more work you put into being good to your physical self, the more emotional and spiritual benefits you'll see. Allow the benefits of physical self-care to guide the holistic cycle of healing your body, mind, and soul.

In the next chapter, we'll look at healing the spirit. We'll learn to empower our creative selves, connect with guides, and set boundaries. We'll figure out the role that our inner selves play in our world, as we embrace magical care of the soul.

CHAPTER

Heal and Awaken Your Spirit

Your spirit is the core of your most genuine, magical self. When the spirit is crushed or repressed—whether through disappointments, loss, our own questionable choices, or abuse and trauma—it impacts every aspect of our being. It's not just our psyche and our soul that are damaged; our bodies respond as well, with bouts of exhaustion, irregular sleep patterns, high blood pressure, and other chronic conditions related to stress. But working with the holistic cycle of mind, body, and soul can heal and awaken your spirit.

With a healthy, whole-hearted spirit, you'll enrich not only your magical power, but also your external relationships with the people you love. You'll become more aware of your world. You'll feel more sensitive to your own needs and those of others. In this chapter, you'll learn how to re-evaluate your own presence in the world, empower your creative spark, work with your ancestral guides, and keep your chakras balanced for a sense of harmony and overall wellness.

Embrace Your Inner Spirit

Your inner spirit is a complex blend of all of your thoughts, feelings, and past experiences. It forms the foundation of your beliefs, and determines how you engage with the rest of the world. Many people are conditioned by the rest of the world to ignore their inner spirits—we're taught to be afraid of seeming too confident, too overwhelming, or too much. Repressing your inner spirit is exhausting and inauthentic, and makes you forget who you are. But most of us do it anyway.

As you learn to embrace your inner spirit, healing from the inside out, your authentic self—the person you become when your actions and words align with your thoughts and ideas—will flow outward. You'll gain awareness, understanding, and clarity of purpose, all of which will add to your exterior charisma. The more people see you as a spiritually well-adjusted being, the more they'll be drawn to you—and the more effort they'll put into their relationships with you.

Your inner spirit responds to your visualizations and intent. If you see yourself as enlightened and powerful, your spirit reacts accordingly. By embracing who you are on the inside, you bring power to your thoughts and ideas—and turn them into reality.

Find the Essence of You

Complete acceptance of your true self is the key to a holistic existence. You probably have one big question about that: How do you figure out who you really are? It's a slow, gradual process. But it all comes down to your ability to accept not only your strengths, but also your flaws and weaknesses.

Most of us have been conditioned to embrace only our strengths, and feel shame over our weaknesses. For instance, you might be proud of your artistic ability but filled with shame over your struggles to manage your finances.

In her book *Daring Greatly*, Brené Brown says that even though others may tell us that we should feel shame or disappointment about our lives, ultimately, those are feelings we impose upon ourselves. Because they're self-inflicted feelings, we're also able to free ourselves from them.

What if your true self accepted that you're imperfect—as we all are—and stopped being troubled by the notion? What if your essence, as a vulnerable and open-hearted individual, was based upon loving who you really are, rather than how others viewed you? Once you love who you are, as a spiritual being, you can knock down the barriers to finding your authentic self.

How Do You Show Up in the World?

Do you wonder what your legacy will be—whether you'll leave a lasting imprint, or if you've had any influence on anybody at all? No one wants to be forgotten or feel insignificant. By healing your spirit—evaluating the way you show up in the world and letting your voice be heard—you can create a legacy of nearly unlimited potential. Use the power of your own spirit to remind yourself that you matter, and by extension, remind others that you have things to say and do.

Here are some ways to examine how you show up in the world.

Examine Your Energy

You've probably had an experience where you were immediately drawn to someone new, or decided you didn't want to be around someone, even though you didn't know them well. You were responding to their energy—and people pick up on your energy, as well.

If you spend each day projecting negative thoughts, others are going to see you as a negative person. On the flip side, if you stay positive, you're going to have more uplifting interactions. Improving your relationships starts with you and the energy you're putting forth.

Take some time to examine what sort of energy you're putting out into the world. Are you constantly finding fault in others, and refusing to take responsibility for your own actions? Or do you look for the good in your world, and the people who inhabit it? Is your glass half empty or half full?

Being an optimist doesn't always just happen naturally. But it's something you can train yourself to do with practice. Start by learning to savor the good things in life—even if they're small. Hold on to the moment and think about how great it makes you feel. Set reminders of things you're looking forward to—put a note on your work calendar marking the day you leave for that beach trip. Write down an inspirational quote to stick on your bathroom mirror. Understand that most people aren't deliberately hurtful—instead, they just don't think. Rather than taking someone's words as a purposeful attack, realize that maybe they had no idea that what they said might be upsetting to you. Surround yourself with people who lift you up rather than drag you down, and you'll be able to do the same for them in return.

Tap into Your Emotions

Emotions are symptoms of the real issues in your life, and if you think about your emotions deeply, they'll offer hints about how to work on those issues. If you're feeling worried because you're stepping outside your comfort zone, the real issue is not the worry; it's that you are afraid to do something unfamiliar. If you feel unhappy because you don't like your appearance, the real issue isn't your looks or your sadness—you've got to tackle your own feelings of inadequacy.

Embracing your emotions can help you connect with your true self. Repressing your emotions and refusing to acknowledge them, however, can lead to spiritual stagnation. Even emotions that cause pain or hurt have value. Think of your emotions as an inner navigation system: They tell you where to go and how to get there. Find a way to learn from them.

Empower Your Creative Self

The human spirit is nurtured by creativity. Whether you write, paint, make music, cook, or do woodworking, creative outlets are good for the soul. There's joy to be found in acts of creation, which allow us to build something new from nothing. They help boost our mood and make us happy. Creativity puts us into a meditative, almost trancelike state, letting us be completely invested in the process. And when we finish, there's a sense of pride in accomplishment.

Doing creative work is a powerful and individualized way to heal your spirit and soul. What you make doesn't have to be perfect. You don't need any prior training, and you don't have to show your creative project to anyone or share it if you don't want to. Simply make regular time to do something creative.

Embrace Your Spiritual Side

No matter what religious background you come from, living spiritually is a choice. It's a way of acknowledging that the divine is present in everyone, and truly believing that the universe—or the gods—has our best interests in mind. When we're not in touch with our spirituality, there can be an emptiness, a feeling that we lack purpose. Embracing your spiritual side permits you to learn who you really are and why you're here, and to develop an open-hearted, generous spirit that you can share with others.

Spirituality Is Different for Everyone

In *The Magic of Thinking Big,* David J. Schwartz asks the question, "What world would it be, if everyone in it were just like me?" Your spiritual journey is a uniquely personal one. For some people, it's found in a weekly fellowship inside a building. For you, it may be more inwardly focused, or may involve meeting up once in a while with people who understand you, and going out into the woods together. The key is that what works for you spiritually isn't going to be the same for everyone else. Just as you wouldn't want someone telling you that your beliefs have no value, others may not like it if you are dismissive of their faith.

Focus your attention on what makes your own spirit soar and sing, and don't worry about what your neighbor is doing for theirs.

Connect with Those Who Came Before You

For practitioners of many magical belief systems today, there's a strong connection to ancestral guides and spirits. Consider working with your kinfolk—biological or otherwise—for guidance and wisdom. Your ancestors, those who came before you and whose influence has carried down to you through generations, want you to be successful. They want you to be happy, because that reflects well upon everyone in the family. If you've never done any genealogy research, start by asking living relatives for information on who your people are. You'll learn how to set up an ancestor shrine later in this chapter.

Spells, Remedies, and Rituals

Are you ready to start working transformative magic to heal your spirit? Try the spells and other practices in this section to set boundaries, embellish your creativity, work with the gods and goddesses of your tradition, and find inspiration that will get you back on track.

POWER OF PERSONAL SPACE SPELL

Are you feeling overwhelmed by the demands of other people? Here's a little secret: your needs matter, too. Sometimes, you've got to set boundaries to heal your spirit; that's not selfishness, it's a radical act of self-preservation. This spell invokes a barrier to remind you that your boundaries deserve respect.

MATERIALS:

A blue candle
Scissors
A small piece of red cardstock paper
A black felt-tip pen or marker
A locket that opens and closes

STEPS:

1. Light the candle. Clear your mind and determine the focus of the boundaries you need to set. Are there people at work who are overstepping? Do you have a family member taking advantage of you?

2. Use the scissors to cut a small octagonal shape out of the card stock—it doesn't have to be perfect. With the marker, write the word STOP across the middle of your octagon. You've just created a stop sign of your own.

3. Hold it in your hands and close your eyes. Say: "It's time to stop, you shall not pass, this is where I draw the line. No more demands shall be made; I reclaim the power that is mine."

4. Fold your stop sign up and tuck it in the locket. Wear it often. And when you encounter people who try to test your limits, visualize that stop sign as a barrier to those who would take advantage of you.

TALISMAN FOR CREATIVITY

In many magical traditions, keys are powerful symbols that open up knowledge, mysteries, and new beginnings. They also unlock the paths to inspiration, ideas, and wisdom. If your creativity feels blocked or out of reach, make this talisman to get your imagination back on track. Do this spell during the waxing moon phase.

MATERIALS:

A shiny new key
A chain
Embellishments like charms or beads (optional)
A white candle
A bowl of soil
A feather
A cup of water

STEPS:

1. String the key on the chain and add your charms or beads to make a necklace.

2. Light the candle.

3. Pass the key over the four representations of the elements and invoke them to give it power. Say: "I call on the powers of earth, to keep me grounded and focused. I call upon the powers of air, to bring me creativity and vision. I call upon the powers of fire, to bring passion and drive to my ideas. I call upon the powers of water, to wash away that which blocks me."

4. Hold the key between your palms and close your eyes. Visualize creative energy flowing through it. Say: "I open my heart, my mind, and my spirit with this key. Creative powers are mine to unlock."

5. Wear your talisman regularly to help open up new ideas and creative thought processes.

Working with Deities

In many of today's witchcraft traditions, practitioners work with gods and goddesses. You may be interested in the deities of a particular pantheon—Celtic, Norse, Yoruba, or others—or you might find yourself honoring a non-specific god and goddess who represent the sacred masculine and the divine feminine. Try offering prayers that ask your deities for assistance with a problem, request advice and guidance, or simply thank them for blessings you've received. Regardless, be sure to treat your deities with respect. A prayer or petition should come from the heart and be sincere and genuine. And once it's granted, **appro** priate gratitude should be shown.

Magical Offering Bowl

For some practitioners of witchcraft, it's common courtesy to present your gods and goddesses with offerings. Since creation is a magical act, crafting your own offering bowl can enhance your spiritual practice.

MATERIALS:

Air-dry clay
Water
Embellishment items like shells or flat stones
A knife or other inscribing tool

STEPS:

1. Mold the clay with your hands and roll it into a ball. Place it on a dry surface and press down gently so that the bottom flattens. Press your thumbs into the center and push down to make a depression.

2. As you push into the clay, begin pulling it outward, stretching and moving it to form a bowl shape. Visualize how you'll use your bowl, and the offerings it will hold. If the clay begins to dry out, dip your fingertips in the water and moisten the surface.

3. Once you're happy with the bowl's design, press embellishments into the clay. Add seashells if you feel connected to the powerful energy of the sea, flat stones to represent the grounding energy of the earth, or even magical crystals of different properties. Use the knife to inscribe magical or sacred symbols on the clay.

4. Allow the clay to dry for at least a week. Then consecrate it by saying: "I bless this bowl that I have made with my own hands. I will use it for the greater good, for higher purpose, and to honor my gods and goddesses. I charge this bowl with power and light."

Use your bowl in ritual and spellwork to make offerings to your deities. These can include herbs, food, drinks, handmade items, or anything else that would be worthy of giving your gods.

Spiritual Booster Incense Blend

Incense can be a powerful booster for any magical working, because the smoke carries your intentions off into the universe, enhancing your spell or ritual. Mix up this spiritual incense blend and burn it to give your healing magic some extra energy. Perform this working in the evening, preferably during a full moon.

MATERIALS:

A small bowl

1 teaspoon frankincense resin

1 teaspoon dried chamomile blossoms

1 teaspoon dried rosemary

1 teaspoon dried mugwort

1 teaspoon dried jasmine flowers

STEPS:

1. Place the frankincense in the bowl, making sure it's crushed into small pieces. Add the herbs, one at a time, stirring gently in a clockwise direction.

2. As you blend the herbs together, envision power and energy infusing them. Say: "Herbs of power, herbs of magic, I blend you together this night."

3. Store your incense blend in a dark-colored glass jar for safekeeping.

> To use, light a charcoal disc—available at any spiritual supply shop—in a fire-safe bowl. When the disc begins to spark, sprinkle a small amount of your loose incense on top, and let it burn. As the smoke rises, say: "I send my intent up into the skies, carrying my magic far and wide."

CHANGING SEASONS SPELL

One of the most powerful ways to heal and awaken your spirit is to develop awareness of the changing seasons. As you start noticing shifts in the air, the soil, the plants, and the skies, you'll gain a new understanding of how your spirit is impacted by your environment and surroundings. Do this spell each month, in the same outdoor location.

MATERIALS:

A journal and pen
A small glass jar with a lid

STEPS:

1. Go to your chosen spot and find a place to sit comfortably. Breathe deeply and regularly. Say: "I open myself to the gifts of the earth and sky, to the awareness of all that surrounds me."

2. Close your eyes and allow your senses to take in everything around you. What do you hear, smell, taste, and feel?

3. Use the journal to write down all the sensations you experienced. How are they different from the last time you were here? What has changed?

4. Before you leave your spot, take a small natural item from the ground—a pebble, a fallen leaf, a seed pod—and place it in the jar. In its place, leave something of your own, such as a piece of hair. Say: "I am connected to this space, I am connected to the earth and sky. I am aware, I am conscious, I am awake."

5. Each month, add another small item to your jar. Keep this collection in your magical workspace, and when you perform spells or rituals, draw on the natural power within the jar.

Make a Witch's Ladder

A witch's ladder is a powerful tool for spellwork and ritual, in which different colors are used to represent intentions. Traditionally, the colors include red, white, and black, as well as feathers in nine different colors. This variant uses white for enlightenment, blue for healing, and purple for power.

MATERIALS:

9 feet each of white, blue, and purple yarn or cord
9 similar items in different colors: buttons, beads, etc.

STEPS:

1. Tie the ends of the three pieces of yarn together and begin braiding. As you do, work the beads or buttons into the yarn, securing them with a knot.

2. As you work, you can say this traditional chant: "By knot of one, the spell's begun. By knot of two, the magic's true. By knot of three, so it shall be. By knot of four, the power's stored. By knot of five, the magic thrives. By knot of six, the spell is fixed. By knot of seven, the future is leavened. By knot of eight, my will is fate. By knot of nine, what's done is mine."

3. As you tie knots, focus your intent on personal empowerment, healing, and enlightenment. When you've completed the braid and added all the beads, knot the end and hang it over your workspace. Use this to meditate or as a counting tool in spellwork.

4. You can make other witch's ladders for different purposes by changing the colors of the yarn.

LITTLE JAR OF INSPIRATION

The word *inspired* means *in spirit*—when you find something that inspires you, it helps you live in a way that brings your spirit joy. If you can experience the joy of inspiration, you'll suddenly find that everything falls into place, just the way it should.

It's often hard to figure out what inspires us, because we live in a world that rarely values inspiration—so instead of feeling inspired, we ignore the things that make us feel spiritually content and whole. This simple method keeps your inspiration nearby, so at a moment's notice, you can grab something to motivate your spirit.

MATERIALS:

A pretty jar with a lid
Acrylic paints, markers, or other art supplies
A notepad and pen

STEPS:

1. Use the paints or marker to decorate the jar in a way that makes you happy. You can write words like "Inspiration," "Ideas," or "Motivation" on it, or just paint designs that inspire you.

2. When you've finished, hold the jar in your hands, and say: "Inspiration come to me, burning brightly in my spirit and soul. Inspiration wait for me, growing greater and more magical over time. Inspiration be ready for me, and my eager, joyful heart."

3. Place the jar somewhere you'll see it regularly, with the notepad and pen. When you have an inspiring idea, jot it down on a slip of paper and add it to the jar.

4. Any time you're feeling a lack of motivation or inspiration, open the jar, pull out a piece of paper, and act on the idea.

CHAKRA BOOSTING CHARM BAG

Many people believe that we draw power from our seven chakras. If one is out of balance, we can feel off-kilter. Create a charm bag to keep your chakra vibrations on an even keel. Do this spell during a full moon, a time associated with wisdom, intuition, and our higher spiritual powers.

MATERIALS:

A white candle

A white cotton drawstring bag

7 small stones to correspond with each chakra, one in each color— for instance: bloodstone, carnelian, citrine, green tourmaline, turquoise, lapis, and amethyst or clear quartz

STEPS:

1. Light the candle and open the bag. Hold the stones in your hands, one at a time, and place them inside the bag.

2. As you add them, invoke the powers of each chakra. Say: "I call balance to the red energy of my root chakra, and my physical needs. I call balance to the orange energy of my sacral chakra, and my emotions. I call balance to the yellow energy of my solar plexus chakra, and my power and vitality. I call balance to the green energy of my heart chakra, bringing me love. I call balance to the blue energy of my throat chakra, and the gift of communication. I call balance to the indigo energy of my brow chakra, embracing my intuition. I call balance to the violet energy of my crown chakra, bringing me understanding."

3. Breathe deeply, focusing on the candle's flame, and imagine balance and harmony throughout your body. Repeat this ritual at each full moon to bring your chakras into alignment as needed.

THE SEVEN CHAKRAS

The concept of chakras comes to us from Eastern traditions. Each chakra, or energy vortex, is a center of spiritual power, in a particular area of the human body, and is associated with specific physical and emotional aspects. When one chakra is blocked or off-balance, you might have problems with the corresponding physical or emotional experience. Our chakras keep the mind, body, and spirit balanced, and when they're open and aligned, we are better able to live as our highest spiritual selves. The chakras are:

- Root (red), at the base of the spine, associated with our relationship to material items.
- Sacral (orange), around the spleen, related to how we connect emotionally to others.
- Solar plexus (yellow), above the navel, focusing on self-empowerment.
- Heart (green), giving us the ability to love and be loved.
- Throat (blue), aiding in communication and matters of trust.
- Brow (indigo), in the center of the forehead, related to intuition.
- Crown (violet), on the top of the head, centered on our sense of purpose, under-standing, and the divine.

ANCESTOR SHRINE

One of the most powerful ways to draw inspiration and power into your spiritual life is by working with your ancestors. You can honor the people who came before you—whether they're kinfolk of the blood or those you've chosen—and ask them for guidance and assistance when you set up a shrine in your home. Be sure never to include images of living people on an ancestor shrine.

MATERIALS:

Any flat surface—a shelf or tabletop will do

Fabric to use as an altar cloth

Photos of your deceased ancestors

Family heirlooms, genealogy charts, or symbols of your heritage

Candles

An offering of food or drink

Essential oil of rosemary, frankincense, or myrrh (optional)

STEPS:

1. Clean the surface of your shrine thoroughly, with a soft towel and some lemon juice or other natural cleaning products, and place the fabric on top of it. You may wish to anoint the corners with essential oil of rosemary, frankincense, or myrrh, all of which are associated with spiritual growth. In some magical traditions, an ancestor shrine always has a white cloth, but use whatever fabric speaks to you.

2. Decorate your shrine with the photos of your loved ones, as well as heirlooms and other symbols, and arrange the candles around them.

3. Light the candles, and present your offering. Say: "Ancestors, loved ones, I call to you and welcome you. Bring me guidance, bring me wisdom, bring me prosperity, bring me hope. I honor you and invite you into my home."

4. If there's something specific you'd like to ask your ancestors for help with, do so. Leave your shrine in place, and whenever you walk by it, acknowledge your people and say hello.

END OF DAY AFFIRMATION

Life can get chaotic and crazy, but that doesn't mean you shouldn't stop to reflect upon what you've learned each day. Wrap up your evening with this simple bedtime affirmation, and use it to map out your plans for the coming day.

MATERIALS:

A blue candle
Lavender sprigs

STEPS:

1. Follow your normal evening routine, but before you climb under the covers, light the candle. Focus on the flame as you sit on the bed.

2. Hold the lavender in your hands, inhaling its gentle, soothing aroma.

3. Say: "I release the negative I gathered today—worry, doubt, and fear. I embrace the good I gathered today—joy, love, and peace. I celebrate the understanding I gathered today—gratitude, wisdom, and knowledge. I will learn from all, and I give myself permission to fall asleep without worry or anxiety. Tomorrow, I will gather good once more."

4. Extinguish the candle and place the lavender under your pillow. Sleep well and welcome the morning as a fresh start.

Conclusion

You're well on your way to transformative healing. With small but radical acts of self-care, you are healing your body, your mind, and your spirit. You're becoming enlightened, awakened, more magical, and more powerful. Now it's time to branch out.

In the next chapter, we'll learn how to take the gift of personal power and use it to heal the community. We'll discuss the power of a group of people, why people have different priorities, the challenges of organizing and working together, and what we can do to help heal our communities, both locally and globally.

Let's get ready to take on the world.

7
CHAPTER

EMBRACE YOUR COMMUNITY

As we've discussed, one of the benefits to radical self-care is that, in addition to healing yourself, you can turn that power outward and use it to help others. As you become more confident, more aware of who you are and your place in the world, you'll discover that *you matter*. And when you matter, you can make a difference in so many things. Why not turn your witchcraft outward, and use what you've learned to heal the community around you?

There's always been a strong connection between magic and activism because, as David Salisbury points out in *Witchcraft Activism: A Toolkit for Magical Resistance*, magic will always respond to a world in crisis. He says witchcraft "screams to be heard because it is the lighthouse for the voiceless." That's pretty powerful, isn't it?

What can you do to make a difference in your community? Learn to understand the root causes of what's broken before you tackle fixing it. Take time to assess the issue at hand, so you know what the real problem is. And then, take action.

Community Means Different Things to Different People

First, it's important to talk about what community means, because every-one has a slightly different definition. For some, it's simply their town or neighborhood. For others, it's got a global feel to it. In general, community means a group of people who share interests, goals, or attitudes. Most of us are part of many different communities, some of which overlap one another, and others are distinctly separate on the Venn diagram of our world.

Define What Community Means to You

How do you view community? Who are the people you share your life with, and how do you interact with them on a regular basis? You have your geo-graphic community—the people who live in your neighborhood, town, or city. You probably also have a spiritual community, made up of like-minded folks with whom you find fellowship. Maybe you're part of a community organized around a specific hobby or activity, like jogging or board games. Perhaps you're involved in communities that revolve around your children—parent-teacher organizations, scouting groups, or club sports activities. Don't discount the importance and value of online communities as well; many of us have deep, rich connections with people we've met via social networking. You're the only one who can define what your community means, but at the end of the day, it's about a group or setting that makes you feel like you belong. It's a sense of *togetherness*.

Friends, Family, Love, and Relationships Near and Far

Your friends and family often form the nucleus of your connection to the world. After all, they're the people you spend the most time with. Although we all value individualism, and the things that make us stand out as unique, it's also important to find a sense of belonging. Through shared collabora-tion, we can build that feeling of being part of something that's bigger than ourselves. Our interactions with those to whom we're the most emotionally linked form a wonderful little world of trust, cooperation, and love, allowing us to work side by side to make our community stronger.

The Benefits of Community

Our communities—however we may define them—play significant roles in every aspect of our lives. As technology continues to expand, connecting us and separating us in equal amounts, it's important to have a sense of belonging. Forming connections helps make us feel less lonely; there are always people who can make you feel like you're a part of a greater whole.

A strong, well-developed community is a place of potential and opportunity. There's always something to focus on, and by working together toward common goals, there's very little that can't get done. Your community doesn't even have to be large. Motivational speaker and minister Norman Vincent Peale said that even with a group of just two, "You can change your life, I can change mine, and together we can change the world around us."

Draw Strength from Those around You

During the coronavirus pandemic of 2020, when this book was being written, there were countless examples of people banding together to lend support to those in need. Health-care workers were exhausted, but communities rallied to support them. Food pantries were overwhelmed by hungry families, yet volunteers worked tirelessly around the clock to staff them.

Suddenly thrust into self-isolation, many people struggled emotionally and mentally. And yet, their friends came together, organizing virtual meetings and group chats, drive-by birthday wishes, and impromptu socially distanced neighborhood sing-alongs. Even in the midst of devastating heartache, those who suffered were able to draw strength from others.

Let Their Support Lift You Up

When you're struggling, you have to be able to turn to your core people. In fact, it's the first place you should look. Your friends and neighbors can be the most powerful sources of inspiration, wisdom, guidance, and healing. Rather than tearing you down, your community should be a group that elevates you. Instead of destroying, your community should help you create.

Who are the people in your circle? Who do you look to for assistance when you need to be pulled out of a pit? In turn, how are you helping others when they're down? You've got knowledge and wisdom of your own that your community members can benefit from, if you take the time to share it. Your community is a rich source of support—and if it's not, find a new one.

Heal as a Group

When communities are damaged, the entire group suffers. Everyone in the circle feels the pain. Whether it's in response to a traumatic event, political dissent, or an overall sense of brokenness, a struggling community can have long-term fallout.

The flip side is that while damage impacts an entire group, so does healing. Community-based healing is a powerful thing. Not only does it heal the whole; it also helps repair the individual parts. Community healing work should be focused with a specific target or goal in mind, and for it to be the most effective, everyone's voices should be heard—particularly those who have been marginalized and oppressed. Learn to listen more than you speak, and you'll be better able to facilitate healing for your community.

The Challenges

Having a sense of community can be incredibly rewarding—and it's not something that happens overnight. It takes a lot of hard work, engagement, and the ability to listen and delegate. Build your community around shared ideas and goals, whether that's based on a need to fix something that's broken or add something that's missing.

When you're doing community work, there are going to be challenges. You'll encounter people who disagree with you—that's human nature—so you'll have to figure out how to communicate respectfully and fairly with them. There are going to be some people who say they want community but don't want to put in any work. You might even discover someone in your community engaging in inappropriate—or even illegal—behavior. Do you know how you'll deal with these issues when they occur? One key to effective community building is to figure out the potential problems you could face and have a strategy in place *before* they happen.

Miscommunication

Remember the game of Telephone you played as a child? One person would start with a sentence like "The pink elephant is drinking tea," and by the time the message reached the twentieth person, it was about a green leopard who was cooking pudding. Unfortunately, miscommunication can be hugely detrimental to community efforts. When there are conflicts, ask yourself if it's a case of miscommunication, rather than deliberate antagonism.

You can help avoid miscommunication by being conscious of a few simple actions. Learn to be clear and concise in expressing your opinions and expectations. Don't assume that other people will just know what you mean. Practice being a good listener who asks for clarification when needed. Think about your words before you speak. Understand that people have different communication styles, and what works well for one might be useless for another.

Misunderstanding

When you have a large group of people working together based on shared goals and ideas, it's really easy to fall into the trap of misunderstanding needs and wants. If you don't address confusion, you're seen as dismissive; then feelings get hurt, and wedges can be driven into your relationships. While it can't be avoided completely, there are a few things you can do in your community to help minimize misunderstandings.

First of all, see your community members as allies, not enemies. You've got a common goal, right? If everyone is heard and validated, you'll be better able to find solutions to problems. Allow yourself to take a break when conflict escalates; once everyone cools down, you can move forward. Try to use non-accusatory language. For instance, instead of saying, "Why isn't anyone helping me with this project?" try "I'd love it if Karen and Chad could lend a hand here, because they always have great ideas."

Different Priorities

When you're working in your community, remember that even with shared goals, not everyone has the same priorities. Let's say you want to focus on food insecurity in your town. You might decide to run a canned goods drive. Your next-door neighbor thinks it's a great idea, but she's busy getting neighborhood garden plots in place so everyone can plant and grow vegetables. You've got the same goals, but you're prioritizing differently. How can you work together?

Also, remember that sometimes, people's priorities are based upon time and resources. Someone who's working two jobs and raising small children may have less availability to commit to the community than someone who is child-free and doesn't have to work. It doesn't make one less interested or involved than the other. It just means that their priorities are different.

Heal Yourself Before You Heal Your Community

Healing yourself has a ripple effect. Each time you open yourself up to more love, more peace, more pleasure, you transform and move closer to the true self that you really want to find. The more you do this, the better you'll be able to heal and help others.

If you're not taking the time to work on healing yourself, you're going to struggle when it comes to healing your community. Forgiving yourself and learning to love who you are isn't going to create world harmony or end global suffering, but what it does do is better enable you to look at problems on a large scale. When you're in pain, it's hard to help others. As you heal and find your freedom, you'll be able to share your gifts with the world around you.

Spells, Remedies, and Rituals

Are you ready to get out there and start doing radical care for your community? This collection of spells, rituals, and other remedies will help you form a foundation for magical activism, community healing work, environmental care, and sweeping social change. Whether you're working on a local level or a global one, you can, as they say, be the change you wish to see in the world.

Spell to Heal the Environment

Nature is held sacred in witchcraft, so you may want to make protecting it a focus of your magical practice. In addition to taking everyday steps to help the environment—like living sustainably, being conscious of your footprint, and not overusing resources—you can also perform magical actions to help support the earth. Perform this spell outside at sunrise.

MATERIALS:

A wooden or clay bowl
Clean soil
A feather
Clean water

STEPS:

1. Place the soil in the bowl, and say: "I call for protection of the land around me."

2. Pass the feather over the bowl of soil, and say: "I call for healing of the air around me."

3. Pour the water into the bowl, and say: "I call for recovery of the water around me."

4. Run your fingers through the damp soil and visualize healing energy flowing into it. Picture the world becoming clear and clean.

5. Say: "By land, sky, and sea, I call for protection, I call for healing, I call for recovery. I will do all within my power to bring about peace, harmony, and healing to our planet."

6. With your fingers, sprinkle the soil around you, and take a moment to envision that healing energy traveling into the earth itself.

Perform this working on the same day and in the same place each month to bring about healing to the environmental space you inhabit.

CIRCLE OF ENERGY RITUAL

Getting people organized to work toward a common purpose is a lot like herding cats. Half of them wander off in different directions, a few get cranky, and one or two just sit down and do nothing. If you're working within a group for community healing, do this ritual with your team, raise some energy, and get everyone focused. This ritual uses chanting, but there are many ways to raise group power; you can also use drumming, dancing, or any other method you like. If possible, perform this rite during the full moon.

MATERIALS:

A bowl of small citrine stones, associated with exploration of new ideas—one for each participant

STEPS:

1. Invite everyone in the group to stand in a circle, joining hands, and place the bowl of citrine crystals in the center. Each participant should close their eyes and visualize energy flowing around the circle, from one person to the next.

2. Begin the chant—you can use this one, or something more appropriate to your group's purpose: "We are a wise family, we are a strong family, we are a whole family, working hand in hand. We are collaborating, we are ever-changing, we are cooperating, working hand in hand."

3. Repeat the chant, getting louder and stronger each time. As the energy builds, visualize it flowing into the citrine crystals. Continue until you've sung through it nine times.

4. Take a few moments to allow everyone to absorb the power of the group. When everyone is ready to release hands, give each person a citrine stone to carry with them.

Working with Land Spirits

Even if you live in an urban environment, there are still age-old spirits of land and place lingering about. The ancient Romans referred to protective beings associated with specific locations, such as sacred springs and holy wells, as *genius loci*. If you want your local land spirits to protect your community, consider making offerings as a way to engage. Do this on a sunny day.

MATERIALS:

An offering appropriate to the area's history and location: grain, water, homemade bread, a stone, flowers, honey, or other locally sourced organic material

STEPS:

1. Get to know the land spirits in your area by listening when you're outside. Breathe deeply, close your eyes, and allow your mind to wander a bit. Are there spots that feel magical, or highly energized? There could be a land spirit there.

2. Once you've identified the spot where your land spirit resides, get in the habit of saying a short prayer or blessing each time you're there. You can say something as simple as "Thank you, brother/sister, for keeping your watchful eye upon this place, and for protecting all of us who call it home. I will work to protect you in return."

3. Leave your offering in a place where it can remain undisturbed— under a tree or bush, near a riverbank, at the corner of a building. When you leave it, say: "I leave this for you to show my gratitude."

> Remember, offerings can include actions as well. Clean up trash in the area or perform other community-focused activities as a way of showing your appreciation.

SECRET EMAIL SIGNATURE SPELL

Sometimes, healing community involves sharing petitions, mailing letters, and sending emails to people with decision-making power. If you're firing off emails to your local city council, why not add a secret spell into your signature to influence their policy?

MATERIALS:

Your laptop and email program

STEPS:

1. Create a simple spell of intention by thinking of one or two words that summarize your purpose, such as "end hunger" or "stop development."

2. Take your word or phrase and eliminate all of the vowels. "End hunger" becomes "nd hngr," while "stop development" turns into "stp dvlpmnt."

3. Get rid of duplicated letters and blend the remaining ones together: "nd hngr" is now "ndhgr," and "stp dvlpmnt" turns into "stpdvlmn."

4. Rearrange the letters any way you like, until you're satisfied with the way they look.

5. Open up your email program's Signature file and enter your name. Paste the string of letters below your name, and then adjust the font color so that the letters are now white. They'll be invisible against the white background any time you send an email.

6. Use this signature file whenever you're sending an email to someone whose decision you hope to influence.

PROTEST PROTECTION TALISMAN

A lot of community work takes place by way of protest; in some cases, it's the only thing that brings about change. Even if you're going to a peaceful protest, it's important to take precautions: bring shatter-resistant eye protection and fresh water, and have a first aid kit handy. Be sure to write your name and emergency contact person's information on your skin in permanent marker. While you're doing that, tuck a protection talisman in your pocket—don't wear it around your neck, because it could be grabbed if things get heated. Do this spell during the full moon.

MATERIALS:

A yellow candle
A piece of yellow amber

STEPS:

1. Light the candle and watch the flame. Say: "I am protected, I am safe, I am aware of my surroundings. Alone or in a crowd, I remain unharmed."

2. Hold the amber in your hands, and visualize protective energy enveloping it. Say: "Wherever I walk, wherever I go, I remain healthy and whole."

3. Blow out your candle. Keep your amber talisman in your pocket if you attend a protest. Be sure to follow standard safety protocols as well.

WITCHCRAFT AND ACTIVISM

As the world changes and evolves, the occult is often a mode of defense and empowerment. Activism and witchcraft go hand in hand. Many formidable acts of resistance have been launched by people who saw them as part of a spiritual calling—and if magic is designed to bring about change, then using it to alter the things that hurt and anger you seems like a logical step. Whether you're working to smash patriarchy, tear down racist institutions, repair the damage caused by global climate change, or bring justice to an unjust world, alchemize your anger, and use it to bring about good.

WINDS OF CHANGE SPELL

What does your community need to do differently? How can you bring about change in your world? Take advantage of a blustery day and send your intention out into the universe. Do this spell during the waning moon phase.

MATERIALS:

A piece of paper
A pen

STEPS:

1. Go someplace where you can see for a long distance around you, such as a hilltop or the roof of a tall building. Stand with your arms outstretched wide, feeling the wind blow around you.

2. On the piece of paper, write down things you want to see eliminated from your community: "racism, hatred, anger, strife, discontent, inequality."

3. Slowly tear the paper into pieces. As you tear, say: "I banish negativity from my community, I banish ill will from my community, I banish discontent from my community. These things I throw to the wind and send away for good."

4. Throw the pieces of paper into the breeze and watch them blow away, as the winds of change whisk negative influences away from your community.

POWER THROUGH UNITY OIL

Mix up a batch of this oil blend and use it to anoint your skin or your magical tools when you're doing community-based rituals and spellwork. If you don't have access to these essential oils, you can substitute other herbs that are associated with power. Find a quiet space to work, where you won't be disturbed.

MATERIALS:

A white candle
A dark-colored glass bottle with a cap
⅛ cup unscented base oil, such as grapeseed or jojoba
6 drops frankincense essential oil
4 drops patchouli essential oil
Pinch powdered clove
Pinch powdered nutmeg

STEPS:

1. Light the candle and focus on the flame for a moment. Say: "I work for a higher purpose, I work for a greater good, I work for something bigger than myself."

2. Pour the base oil into the bottle and add the essential oils. Blend by swirling gently in a clockwise direction.

3. Add the clove and nutmeg, and swirl some more until thoroughly blended. As you do, visualize power and unity bringing your group together for a common purpose or goal, or based upon shared interests. Imagine the oils and powders mixing together, working in harmony, just like the people in your community.

4. Be sure to label the bottle with the ingredients and date. Dab a bit on your wrists when you're about to meet other people in your community, on your shoes if you head out to pound the pavement, or on your magical tools when you're doing unity-focused workings.

Be a Good Ally

Feminist writer Laurie Penny says the amount of anger a woman is permitted to express is directly proportional to her social status—and she's right. If you come from a place of privilege, whether it's related to your skin color, gender, or income level, it's important to be a good ally to people who might not have the same advantages you do. The best allies are the ones who don't have to be the center of attention. Be sure you:

- Use inclusive language.
- Honor people's pronouns and gender identity.
- Acknowledge that your experiences are different from other people's.
- Step back from the spotlight and let marginalized voices be heard.
- Check your unconscious behaviors that negatively impact others.

FLAG SPELL FOR COMMUNITY

No matter what community you're a part of, there's a good chance there's a flag to represent it. Perhaps you identify simply as an American, flying the stars and stripes, or a resident of a particular municipality, waving your state or city flag. Maybe you're part of the LGBTQ+ community, a spiritual community, or a group with some other shared interest. If you're part of a group that doesn't have a flag, make your own with fabric and paint, or even with paper and markers or crayons. Do this spell during the waxing moon phase to attract unity to your group.

MATERIALS:

A flag to represent your community
Power through Unity Oil (page 130)
A flagpole or other place to display your flag

STEPS:

1. Fold your flag into a triangle.

2. Anoint the three corners with a dab of Power through Unity Oil, and say: "Friends and neighbors, work with me, side by side as community. I call my people both near and far, our community is part of who we are. I call for unity, with harm to none, this flag will wave while we heal as one."

3. Display your flag with pride so your friends, neighbors, and community members will see it and be influenced by your working. If you're concerned that displaying a flag publicly will cause problems or endanger you, you can tuck it into an unobtrusive spot inside your front door rather than hanging it outside, so that visitors will pick up on its energy when they enter your home.

ELEMENTAL RITUAL TO BLESS DONATIONS

If you've gathered donations to help your community, it's a great idea to bless them before passing them along—giving is a sacred act, so anything that you're donating should be treated as spiritual. When you bless them with the elements, you remove any negative energy that might be contained within, and infuse them with positive, generous intentions. Whether it's canned foodstuffs, clothing, or cash in hand, do this ritual invoking the elements before donating.

MATERIALS:

All of your donated goods
A white candle
Symbols of the four elements, such as a dish of soil, a feather or
   fan, a small tealight, and a dish of water

STEPS:

1. Place your donated items and the candle in the center of your workspace, with the elemental symbols in their appropriate directional locations: earth at the northernmost point, air to the east, fire in the south quadrant, and water represented in the west.

2. Move toward your symbol of the north, saying, "Powers of Earth! I call to you to bless this donation, granting strength to those who receive."

3. Approach the east and say: "Powers of Air! I call you to bless this donation, whispering the breath of kindness into those who give."

CONTINUED

ELEMENTAL RITUAL TO BLESS DONATIONS

4. When you get to the south, say: "Powers of Fire! I call you to bless this donation, burning passion into those who bring positive change."

5. Finally, approach the west. Say: "Powers of Water! I call you to bless this donation, washing away any negativity, and filling these items with love."

6. Light the candle, and say: "I bless these donations for my community, that others may benefit from what I contribute. There is no shame in need, no inferiority in want, and I give freely of my heart to those who would benefit from aid."

7. Take some time to meditate on how your donations will help others. When you're ready, drop them off where they're most needed.

Public Speaking Power Spell

Speaking in public can be downright terrifying. There are a few actions you can take to prepare, like practicing your speech, staying focused, and doing enough research on your topic to become an expert on the subject matter. But you might still feel nervous. This tea spell, brewed from herbs associated with the throat chakra, will help you feel a little more confident when it's time to deliver—and you'll be better prepared to think on your feet if someone asks you unexpected questions.

MATERIALS:

1 cup water
1 teaspoon dried chamomile
1 teaspoon peppermint
1 teaspoon borage
Cloth teabag or a tea strainer

STEPS:

1. Bring the water to a boil.

2. While it's heating up, place the dried herbs in the teabag or strainer and place it in a mug.

3. Pour the boiling water over the herbs and allow them to steep for 10 minutes.

4. Remove the teabag and sit down to drink your tea. While you do, practice your speech. Quiz yourself on key talking points; you may even want to do this in a mirror if it helps you.

5. As you sip, pay attention to the tea as it warms your throat chakra, and focus on being more confident and speaking with authority.

6. When it's time for you to speak in public, remember the comforting sensation of the tea in your throat, and deliver your words with confidence and style.

Conclusion

Healing your community is a powerful action. As the world around you heals and becomes stronger, you'll continue to grow as an individual. With shared goals and cooperative, collaborative activities, you can expand your reach throughout your world—whether it's a single corner of your street, your entire city, or beyond.

In the next chapter, we'll look at healing at home. By making your personal space a sanctuary of peace, harmony, and safety, you'll create an environment in which you can retreat from the world and work on self-development and personal growth. You'll learn spells for clearing negative energy from your house, creating and protecting your personal safety zone, and finding healthy, joyful ways to reflect upon your space.

When your home is welcoming, warm, and harmonious, you'll find it even easier to work on personal self-care within its walls.

Make Your Home Your Sanctuary

Your home should be a relaxing retreat from the world. It's where you spend most of your time, alone or with the people you love. It's a sacred and special place where you can relax, feel safe, and be comfortable. It's not about the things you have in your home; it's about how you feel when you're there. The decisions you make and actions you take in your home have a direct impact on how you interact with the rest of the world once you step outside your front door.

In this chapter, you'll learn how to create a sacred space in your own home, eliminate negativity, and craft an environment that's warm and welcoming as you work toward healing, abundance, and joy.

The Role of the Home

Your home serves a purpose beyond being where you sleep at night and store your clothes. It ought to create a sense of place that centers us and keeps us grounded. Graham Rowles, a gerontology professor at the University of Kentucky, says, "There is pretty strong evidence that the environment in which people live is closely linked to their well-being."

The home is a place enriched by memories—both positive and negative ones—and creates an emotional attachment for the future. By turning your home into a place of familiarity and comfort, you can reduce your own stress levels and enhance your overall happiness.

A Safe Retreat from the World

Life often gets chaotic and out of control, whether it's the stress of work or dealing with global issues and politics. Why not turn your home into a safe space where you can retreat when everything becomes too much? Whether you live in a small apartment or a sprawling house in the suburbs, your home can provide you with a sense of escape. Focus on comfort—find furniture you love to sit on. Fill your home with things that bring you joy— art, candles, music, big squishy pillows, or plants. Make it the sort of place where you breathe a big sigh of relief after a hectic workday, because you know you've just stepped into your happy place.

A Place That Reflects You

Do you ever feel like you're just occupying a space, rather than living in it? Turn your home into a place that reflects who you are. Paint walls in colors you love. Fill shelves with your favorite books. Hang photos of your family. Add artwork that speaks to you. Do you have a collection of something that is meaningful to you? Display it so you can see it every day. Select furniture that aligns with your lifestyle—are you more structured and formal, or is your family casual and rough-and-tumble? Make the rooms work for you— if you'd rather eat in the kitchen and you never use that big dining room, why not turn it into a library or office? Show off your accomplishments, like trophies and diplomas. Allow your home to showcase your unique and magical personality.

A Creative Outlet

Your home should also be a place where you can create. Do you write, draw, or make music? Maybe you express your creativity in other ways. Regardless, let your house or apartment stimulate and nurture your creative spirit. If you've got the space and the resources, set up a spot where you can create. Even if your creative work takes place at a small desk in a corner or an easel by the window, the ability to create something from nothing is powerful. Once you've created something—whether it's a painting, a new knitted blanket, or a wood carving—display your work proudly in your home so you can enjoy the fruits of your imaginative labor and feel inspired to produce more.

The Importance of Home as a Healing Space

The home also serves a valuable function as a healing space. Creating an environment conducive to healing is part of the holistic approach to self-care. Think about the shapes, colors, and textures in your home. Do they bring you joy and make you feel relaxed, or do they induce anxiety and apprehension? Spaces that are cluttered, noisy, and chaotic can lead to stress and frustration, but a place of comfort and quiet reflection can boost your well-being.

Spells, Remedies, and Rituals

Are you ready to work on making your home a sanctuary of your very own? This collection of spells, rituals, and other remedies features ways that you can eliminate negative energy from your personal space, create magic in your garden, do a bit of decluttering, and craft an environment that makes you feel positive and safe. Let's get started on making a magical home.

BANISH NEGATIVITY

In many traditions of witchcraft, the broom is a powerful tool. It's not only symbolic, it's effective, because it doesn't just clean your house physically. It also creates a metaphysical cleansing process. Do this spell at sundown during the waning moon phase.

MATERIALS:

Equal parts dried rosemary, sage, lavender, and hyssop
A wooden or clay bowl
A broom

STEPS:

1. One at a time, add the herbs to the bowl. Use your fingers to gently mix them together.

2. As you mix, say: "Herbs of magic, herbs of power, keep my happy home safe and clean."

3. Beginning at your front door, walk around the interior of your home in a clockwise direction. Use your broom to sweep lightly along the perimeter of the floor, at the base of the walls.

4. As you work, say: "Sweep and brush, brush and sweep, negative I banish, blessings I keep."

5. When you get back around to the door, open it and sweep out any detritus you've gathered.

6. Step outside and sprinkle the herbs across your threshold, repeating: "Herbs of magic, herbs of power, keep my happy home safe and clean."

PROPERTY PROTECTION MAGIC

One of the best ways to make your home a place of peace and harmony is to protect it from those who might want to cause harm. Iron is known as a valuable protective element, and the use of nails for protection is found in many forms of folk magic. Some traditions suggest pounding one into the main beam of your home, hammering it into a fence post outside, or even burying one under your front steps.

MATERIALS:

4 heavy iron nails
A heavy mallet
4 silver dimes

STEPS:

1. Beginning at the northernmost corner of your property, use the mallet to pound a nail into the ground. As you do, say: "None shall pass that will do me harm, this property is mine, and I claim it as so."

2. Place a dime on the top of the nail, and say: "I invest in my land, I make it my own, I give this property my energy and spirit, and none shall enter against my will."

3. Cover the nail with loose soil, making sure it's completely buried. Repeat this at the other corners of your property, working in a clockwise direction.

If you don't have your own yard—for instance, if you live in an apartment or dormitory—do this spell by placing a nail and dime in each interior corner of your home.

DECLUTTERING RITUAL

There are plenty of ways to declutter your space, and all of them involve eliminating things that no longer serve you. It does take a bit of a commitment to getting organized, but by taking steps to get rid of things you don't want, don't use, or that don't fit, you can keep clutter out of your house. The less clutter you have, the more room you have for things that make you happy and invite positivity. Do this spell over 13 days, during the waning moon phase.

MATERIALS:

A pink pillar candle—pink is associated with gratitude
A knife or other inscribing tool
13 empty bags or boxes

STEPS:

1. Use the knife to mark horizontal lines on the candle, dividing it into 13 equal segments.

2. Each day, light the candle, and take one bag and walk through your home. You may find it easier to select a single room to work in. Go through closets, dressers, and cabinets, and see what you have.

3. Look at every item you own. Ask yourself: "Do I love this? Do I need this? Does this have value to me?" For clothing, think about whether you've worn it in the past twelve months, and whether it still fits properly.

CONTINUED

DECLUTTERING RITUAL

4. If the answer to the above questions is no, hold the item in your hand. Think about how much you loved it when it first came into your life. Say: "I thank you for being in my life, I release you from service, and I now send you away to be loved by others."

5. Place the item in the bag and repeat with the next object. Once the bag is full, tie it shut and stop for the day. Allow the candle to burn down to the line you've inscribed, and then extinguish it.

6. Do this until all thirteen bags are full. After you've filled all of the bags, do the Elemental Ritual to Bless Donations in chapter 7, and take them to a local donation center.

Keep a separate bag or box for trash, to dispose of things that can't or shouldn't be rehomed.

JUNK DRAWER DIVINATION MAGIC

Do you have a junk drawer or box in your house containing all kinds of randomly accumulated stuff? Divination can be uniquely personal, and often, we get messages that are focused on the environment around us. Pull items from your junk drawer to see the information your house wants you to know.

MATERIALS:

A drawer or box full of random unrelated items

A notebook and pen

A silver candle, which is associated with divinatory magic and intuitive gifts

Your favorite spiritual incense blend

STEPS:

1. Go through your junk drawer to see what's in it. Assign divinatory meanings to each item, and write these meanings down in your notebook. For instance, a pen might represent communication or creativity. Staples or paper clips could symbolize holding things together. Keys and locks can indicate opening up things that were once closed, and loose coins might be omens of coming prosperity. Use your imagination.

2. Once you've written down all of your divinatory meanings, light the candle and incense. Take a deep breath and clear your mind, opening yourself up to messages from your home.

CONTINUED

JUNK DRAWER DIVINATION MAGIC

3. Close your eyes. Extend your dominant hand into the drawer and mix everything up.

4. Without opening your eyes, pull out three individual items.

5. Look to see what they are and check their divinatory meanings. What could your house be trying to tell you?

6. When you're finished, thank your house for its messages and extinguish the candle.

Honor Your Household Guardians

In many ancient cultures, each house had a unique set of guardian spirits. Acknowledging the guardian beings of your home will bring blessings and protection into your family's life. Do you have a particular area in your house or apartment that *feels* special and magical? That may be where your household guardian resides. Some people name their guardians—try asking your house what its guardian wishes to be called. The first name that pops into your head is often the right one. If you've given your guardian a name, use it in this ritual, which you should try to perform regularly.

MATERIALS:

A small altar: a shelf, section of kitchen counter, spot on your hearth, or table
Altar cloth
Statues or images representing your household spirits
A white candle
Your favorite incense
Offerings of food and a beverage
A plate and cup

STEPS:

1. Place the cloth on your altar, arranging the statues or images however you like.

2. Light the candle, and say: "I light this flame in honor of my household guardians. May you protect this house and light our path to blessings."

CONTINUED

HONOR YOUR HOUSEHOLD GUARDIANS

3. Light the incense. Say: "I light this incense in honor of my household guardians. May you look favorably upon our house and send away any negative influences."

4. Place your offerings on the cup and plate. Say: "I offer this food and drink in honor of my household guardians. May you never hunger, may you never thirst."

5. Take a moment to silently reflect upon your household's guardian spirits. When you are ready, say: "Guardians, I thank you for watching over this home and for your blessings upon it. May you be well, and know you are valued."

6. Leave the offerings in place for 24 hours. Dispose of them by pouring the beverage outside near your front door and scattering or burying the food in your yard.

Healing Spaces Outside the Home

Thanks to our busy schedules, we often spend time somewhere other than our homes. Whether you're in your car, office, or classroom, try some of these simple, subtle bits of healing magic to keep yourself balanced and whole when away from home.

- Include symbols of the four elements—earth, air, fire, and water—in a decorative jar or bowl on your desk. Consider a bit of soil or small stones from a favorite location to represent earth, a feather or seed pod as a symbol of air, an unlit candle as a stand-in for fire, and seashells or a cup to represent water.
- Place crystals in discreet corners around your workspace: hematite for protection, amethyst for healing, and rose quartz for positivity.
- Carry a pocket talisman enchanted with magical energy.
- Hang protective charms, such as a pentagram, ankh, or eye talisman, over your car's rearview mirror.

HOME BLESSING OIL

To bring healing, abundance, and overall blessings into your home, blend up a batch of this oil. You can use it to anoint your magical tools and sacred objects, or to dress candles during spellwork for home-focused magic.

MATERIALS:

A blue candle
A dark-colored glass bottle with a cap
⅛ cup unscented base oil, such as grapeseed or jojoba
6 drops sandalwood oil
4 drops jasmine essential oil
4 drops rosemary essential oil
2 drops juniper berry oil

STEPS:

1. Light the candle and focus on the flame for a moment. Say: "I call for protection, I call for security, I call for this home to be blessed."

2. Pour the base oil into the bottle and add the essential oils. Blend by swirling gently in a clockwise direction. Imagine them blending together, working to keep your home safe and harmonious.

3. Be sure to label the bottle with the ingredients and date, and use it regularly to bring blessings into your home. Rub a few drops on your furniture, doors and windows, or even the corners of important family documents.

A Fort for When You Just Can't

Sometimes, the world is just too much. It's okay to want some time to yourself. The opportunity to focus on radical self-care includes actions that nurture the soul and the spirit—sometimes being alone is a great way to do that. This spell is a simple one that you'll want to do when there's no one home to pester you.

MATERIALS:

A couch with cushions
Pillows and blankets
Coloring books
Crayons or colored pencils
Snacks (optional)

STEPS:

1. Pull the cushions off the couch, and arrange them, along with the pillows and blankets.

2. Build yourself a fort, just like you did when you were a kid. Make your fort as fancy or simple as you like. Want a tower? Stack those cushions! How about a skylight? Leave a gap between the blankets.

3. Place your coloring books and crayons inside. Sit on the floor outside your fort and peek through the doorway. Say: "This is my sanctuary, my quiet place. No one will bother me, in this peaceful space."

4. Climb into your fort, make yourself comfortable, and begin coloring. Eat snacks if you want to.

5. Allow yourself the luxury of solitude in a world that doesn't really value silence, and enjoy your afternoon of peace and quiet and coloring.

The Value of Solitude

Our world is hectic, busy, and loud, so there's a lot to be said for finding comfort in solitude. Being alone is different from being lonely, which is marked by a negative sense of involuntary isolation. Choosing to be alone, and embracing solitude, can lead to a positive shift in your self-awareness. Successfully navigating solitude can be done if you:

- Learn to love hanging out with yourself and feel comfortable in your own skin.
- Develop skills and find activities that don't require anyone else's input.
- Spend time embracing your own thoughts.
- Don't let yourself feel bad about being alone.
- Choose to be fully present with others when you return to social activities.

While loneliness can be soul-crushing, solitude often restores the spirit.

Garden Magic

Gardening is a magical activity that brings a sense of tranquility and calm to your life. If you're planting herbs and vegetables, you have the added bonus of growing your own food and magical supplies. Perform this ritual outside, when it's safe for plants to go into the ground in your planting zone, or use it as a way to start your seedlings in a container garden or window planter.

MATERIALS:

A garden, or pots of soil if you don't have a yard
Gardening tools: shovel, trowel, etc.
Seedlings, or seed packets
Water

STEPS:

1. Prepare the soil for planting by tilling, mulching, or whatever you need to do.

2. As you turn the earth over, visualize your seeds taking root in the ground. Feel the elements of nature around you—the cool soil beneath your feet, the breeze on your skin, the warm sun on your face. Connect with the land, and the planet itself.

3. Say: "Today I honor the earth by planting the seeds of life deep within the soil. May this garden grow strong, fertile, and abundant, bringing bounty to my home."

CONTINUED

GARDEN MAGIC

4. Put your seeds or seedlings into the soil, one at a time. With each one, offer this blessing after you dig its hole: "May the soil be blessed, may this plant be blessed, may my home be blessed, bringing life forward and new." Pat the loose soil around the seed and move on to the next one.

5. After all of your seeds are in the ground, water the soil. While you do this, say: "I honor my land by planting these seeds. I will tend it and treat it, keeping this garden healthy, so that my family may eat of its blessings." Visualize your garden blooming and blossoming, full of fresh, healthy herbs and vegetables.

6. Be sure to tend your garden regularly so it will yield healthy plants for you.

Money-Drawing Door and Floor Wash

In many traditions of witchcraft, washes for floors, doors, and windows are used around the home for magical purposes. If you've got bills to pay, want to start saving, or just need a little extra cash in hand, blend this wash to keep things clean and attract money to your home. Do this working on a Friday, or whatever day of the week you normally get paid.

MATERIALS:

1 quart water
1 tablespoon dried bay leaves
1 tablespoon bayberry
1 tablespoon basil
1 tablespoon cloves
1 tablespoon thyme
1 gallon hot water
¼ cup white vinegar
2 gold candles

STEPS:

1. Bring the quart of water to a rolling boil and add the herbs. Allow them to boil for 15 minutes.

2. Turn off the heat, let the herbs steep for an hour, and then strain them out. Discard them outside in your yard.

3. To use the wash, pour into a gallon of hot water and add the vinegar.

CONTINUED

Money–Drawing Door and Floor Wash

4. Light the gold candles, and place one at the back of your house and one at the front. Wash your floors (or spritz it on carpet if you don't have hard floors) from the rear of your home to the front door, being sure to use strokes that move toward you rather than away from you.

5. As you clean your floors, envision money coming into your house. When finished, pour the remaining water outside.

> You can use this wash to spray furniture, clean windows, and wipe down doors as well.

PEACEFUL PROSPERITY INCENSE BLEND

Your home is a sanctuary, and this incense blend will help reinforce that. Blend this incense to use either as an accent to your financial-focused or household-based magic, or simply to burn on its own to bring about a sense of tranquility, peace, and prosperity. Do this working during the waxing moon phase.

MATERIALS:

Equal parts dried lavender, mistletoe, patchouli, pennyroyal, rosemary
A bowl
A dark-colored glass jar
A charcoal incense disc
A fire-safe plate or dish

STEPS:

1. Place the herbs in the bowl, one at a time, making sure they're crushed into small pieces. Begin stirring gently in a clockwise direction.

2. As you blend the herbs together, envision prosperity infusing them.

3. Say: "Herbs of bounty, herbs of blessing, I blend you together to bring abundance to my home."

4. Store your incense blend in a dark-colored glass jar for safekeeping.

5. To use, light a charcoal incense disc in a fire-safe dish. When the disc starts to spark, sprinkle a small amount of your loose incense on top, and let it burn.

6. As the smoke rises, say: "I call bounty, I call abundance, I call prosperity, drawing blessings into my life."

Conclusion

Your home is—or should be—the place where you find comfort and solace. As you're working on healing magic to make your home a sanctuary and a space of joy, ask yourself some important questions. What do you need to bring yourself a sense of tranquility? What are some of the material items or design aesthetics that make your heart soar and inspire your creativity? Leave your signature on your home, from floors to walls to ceiling. Eliminate the negative and welcome positive energy in. Claim your space as your own, by clearing out clutter and detritus, turning it from just a place to keep your stuff into one in which you actually *live*, and opening up your rooms to welcome calm, peace, and healing for everyone who lives there.

Final Thoughts

There are so many magical ways to heal yourself. By introducing healing witchcraft and radical self-care into your regular routine, you can enhance not only your personal life, but also the world around you.

Consider your radical self-care journey for a moment: What do you hope to achieve? What do you want to heal? What aspects of yourself will benefit from taking the time to work transformative magic? Learning to take care of who you are from the inside out, by setting healthy boundaries and reclaiming your own joy, is one of the most revolutionary actions you can take, because there will always be people out there telling you that you don't deserve to be happy—that you're too much, or that you're not enough.

But guess what? The haters don't deserve space in your head, and they don't deserve a place in your arena, because they're not doing the work. You are the only one who can make the choice to move toward radical self-care and healing. And when you do finally make that commitment to yourself, you are going to be mighty.

You'll develop stronger, richer relationships with the people in your life, and as you do, you'll benefit from the powerful actions of a holistic approach to empowerment. Give yourself the luxury and the privilege of healing your mind, body, and soul, as well as your community and the whole world. Let other people see you for who you really are—your authentic, genuine, powerful self—and they'll respond accordingly. Above all, treat yourself like the magical, worthy, uniquely incredible being that you are. You deserve it.

RESOURCES

Are you interested in learning more about witchcraft and magical practice? Here are some great resources you'll want to check out for additional information and insight:

Blake, Deborah: *Everyday Witchcraft: Making Time for Spirit in a Too-Busy World* (Llewellyn, 2005). Learn to walk your path with style and wisdom by dedicating a few minutes of each day to spiritual growth and development.

Cunningham, Scott: *Encyclopedia of Magical Herbs* (Llewellyn, 1985). This is the gold standard for anyone interested in herbal magic, and describes nearly 500 herbs and plants that can be used in spellwork and ritual.

Iles, Judika: *Encyclopedia of Witchcraft: The Complete A–Z for the Entire Magical World* (HarperOne, 2014). This fantastic compendium covers history, folklore, mythology, and a collection of celebrations, spells, and rituals.

IncitingARiot.com: This pagan podcast features authors and academics who are experts in a variety of magical and occult topics.

Morrison, Dorothy: *The Craft: A Witch's Book of Shadows* (Llewellyn, 2001). Take a refreshing look at traditional witchcraft, including spells, rituals, celebrations, and magical theory.

Murphy-Hiscock, Arin: *The Green Witch: Your Complete Guide to the Natural Magic of Herbs, Flowers, Essential Oils, and More* (Adams Media, 2017). Learn about the healing properties of magical plants in this easy-to-use but in-depth study.

PaganSquare.com: This is an online community where witches, pagans, and other practitioners can safely interact and share topics relevant to their beliefs and practices.

Patheos.com/pagan: Part of the Patheos network of spiritual blogs and sites, the Pagan channel is chock-full of articles by witchcraft practitioners from communities and cultures around the world.

REFERENCES

Brown, Brené. *Daring Greatly: How the Courage to Be Vulnerable Transforms the Way We Live*. New York: Penguin Random House, 2015.

Gardner, Gerald Brosseau. *Witchcraft Today*. Secaucus, NJ: Citadel Press, 1954.

Goto, Yasuaki, Shinya Hayasaka, Shigeo Kurihara, and Yosikazu Nakamura. "Physical and Mental Effects of Bathing: A Randomized Intervention Study." *Evidence-Based Complementary and Alternative Medicine*, 2018 (July 2018): 1–5. doi.org/10.1155/2018/9521086.

Grey, Peter. *Apocalyptic Witchcraft*. London, England: Scarlet Imprint, 2013.

Hutton, Ronald. *The Triumph of the Moon: A History of Modern Pagan Witchcraft*. Oxford: Oxford University Press, 2001.

Kondo, Marie. *The Life-Changing Magic of Tidying Up*. Berkeley: Ten Speed Press, 2014.

Lazar, Sara W., Catherine E. Kerr, Rachel H. Wasserman, Jeremy R. Gray, Douglas N. Greve, Michael T. Treadway, Metta Mcgarvey, et al. "Meditation Experience Is Associated with Increased Cortical Thickness." *NeuroReport* 16, no. 17 (2005): 1893–97. doi.org/10.1097/01.wnr.0000186598.66243.19.

Murphy-Hiscock, Arin. *The Witch's Book of Self-Care: Magical Ways to Pamper, Soothe, and Care for Your Body and Spirit*. New York: Adams Media, 2018.

Peale, Norman Vincent. *The Power of Positive Thinking*. New York: Wings Books, 1992.

Penny, Laurie. *Bitch Doctrine: Essays for Dissenting Adults*. London: Bloomsbury Publishing, 2018.

Rowles, Graham D., and Miriam Bernard. *Environmental Gerontology: Making Meaningful Places in Old Age*. New York: Springer Publishing Company, 2013.

Salisbury, David. *Witchcraft Activism: A Toolkit for Magical Resistance*. Newburyport, MA: Weiser Books, 2019.

Schwartz, David J. *The Magic of Thinking Big*. New York: Fireside Books, 1987.

Tausiet, María. "Healing Virtue: *Saludadores* versus Witches in Early Modern Spain." *Medical History* 53, no. S29 (2009): 40–63. doi.org/10.1017/s0025727300072392.

Thompson, Catharine Ward, Jenny Roe, Peter Aspinall, Richard Mitchell, Angela Clow, and David Miller. "More Green Space Is Linked to Less Stress in Deprived Communities: Evidence from Salivary Cortisol Patterns." *Landscape and Urban Planning* 105, no. 3 (2012): 221–29. doi.org/10.1016/j.landurbplan.2011.12.015.

Whaley, Leigh. "The Wise-Woman as Healer: Popular Medicine, Witchcraft and Magic." *Women and the Practice of Medical Care in Early Modern Europe, 1400–1800*, 2011, 174–95. doi.org /10.1057/9780230295179_10.

Wong, Y. Joel, Jesse Owen, Nicole T. Gabana, Joshua W. Brown, Sydney Mcinnis, Paul Toth, and Lynn Gilman. "Does Gratitude Writing Improve the Mental Health of Psychotherapy Clients? Evidence from a Randomized Controlled Trial." *Psychotherapy Research* 28, no. 2 (March 2016): 192–202. doi.org/10.1080/10503307.2016.1169332.

Wright, Katherine. "The Origins and Development of Ground Stone Assemblages in Late Pleistocene Southwest Asia." *Paléorient* 17, no. 1 (1991): 19–45. doi.org/10.3406/paleo.1991.4537.

Glossary

altar: A sacred workspace where magic and ritual take place

amulet: A natural object consecrated and then used for magical purposes

base oil: An unscented and unflavored oil to which essential oils are added

Book of Shadows: A magical book containing the practitioner's spells, rituals, and other information; sometimes referred to as a grimoire

correspondence: The way an item represents another item or concept by way of magical properties

divination: Seeing things to come, by way of mystical or supernatural means

grimoire: A magical book containing the practitioner's spells, rituals, and other information; sometimes referred to as a Book of Shadows

incantation: A chant said during the preparation or performance of a spell

incense: Burning resins, herbs, or plants for their magical properties

magical intention: The purpose for which a spell or ritual is performed

pendulum: A weighted item on a chain or string, used for simple divination spells and rituals

poppet: A doll used in magic to represent the individual for whom the spell is intended

scrying: A form of divination in which the practitioner gazes into a reflective surface, such as water or crystal

talisman: An object that has been enchanted with magical powers

waning moon: The lunar phase in which the moon fades from full back to dark, or new

waxing moon: The lunar phase in which the moon grows from new, or dark, to full

visualization: Focusing the mind to see the ultimate purpose that is desired

INDEX